HAUNTING ILLINOIS

HAUNTING ILLINOIS

A Tourist's Guide to the Weird and
Wild Places of the Prairie State

Second Edition

by

Michael Kleen

Thunder Bay Press

Holt, MI

Haunting Illinois
By Michael Kleen

Copyright © 2011 Michael Kleen

All rights reserved. No part of this book may be reproduced in any form or by any means including photocopying, recording, or by any information storage and retrieval system, without written permission from the copyright owner, except for the inclusion of brief quotations in an article or review.

Originally published 2010
Haunting the Prairie
ISBN: 978-0-9790401-4-6
Black Oak Press
Rockford, Illinois

Second edition published 2011
Thunder Bay Press
Holt, Michigan 48842

First Printing April 2011

15 14 13 12 11   1 2 3 4 5

ISBN: 978-1-933272-29-0

Library of Congress Control Number: 2011926233

Icons by Heather Howard
All interior photos by Michael Kleen
Front cover photo by Rachel Black
Book and Cover Design by Michael Kleen

Printed in the United States of America
By McNaughton & Gunn, Inc.

PRAISE FOR THE FIRST EDITION

"Michael Kleen is for my money the most honest and constantly engaged folklorist in Illinois today. His always careful but never stodgy fleshing-out of beloved legends and twice-told tales is a model for anyone attempting to find the truth without killing the 'spirit' of the stuff we love: the richly magical side of our cherished history."

- Ursula Bielski, author of Chicago Haunts, More Chicago Haunts, and Chicago Haunts 3

"This book has become one of my most valuable resources for planning graveyard expeditions throughout the state of Illinois. Kleen's background as a historian and excellent research skills have enabled him to uncover dozens of obscure sites that have escaped the notice of other authors. The book provides a much-needed geographical balance, highlighting haunted sites and local legends in areas of the state neglected by other researchers."

- Matt Hucke, author of Graveyards of Chicago

"Haunting The Prairie is a chillingly entertaining collection of popular ghost folklore and strange phenomena of Illinois that has been recanted in hushed voices from generations past. It is a pleasurable read for fans of the macabre."

- Peggy Clydesdale, Ghosttraveller.com

"It doesn't take long, paging through Michael Kleen's Haunting the Prairie, to come to the understanding that the future of Illinois folklore is in very capable hands as long as Kleen is at the helm. He artfully and passionately scours the entire state of Illinois, finding interesting and horrifying tales that somehow, until now, were confined to their local boundaries. Kleen throws the curtains open on these rare diamonds in the rough and allows these more remote stories to breath and share the same space as their more famous contemporaries..."

- Scott Markus, author of Voices from the Chicago Grave

"Haunting the Prairie by Michael Kleen is one of the very best books about Illinois paranormal sites that I have ever read. For someone interested in visiting mysterious places in Illinois, this is the book for you. This book tells small town ghost stories many people have not heard before... I highly recommend this book to all Little Egypt Ghost Society members and anyone else interested in exploring the unknown."

- BRUCE L. CLINE, L.E.G.S.

"Michael Kleen's book Haunting the Prairie is a wonderful resource for ghost hunters and paranormal enthusiasts, whether experienced or new in the field. I teach a college class on the paranormal, and this is at the top of my list of recommended books for my students."

- CARL JONES, Lincoln Land Community College

"Michael Kleen gets a kick out of ghost stories and he's willing to travel to see if there's any truth to these legends."

- THE TIMES (Streator)

"Michael Kleen's Haunting the Prairie is the Rand McNally of the paranormal in the State of Illinois. As a paranormal investigator I use it extensively in selecting locations to investigate. I recommend this book to anyone who has an interest in the paranormal and exploring the unknown, whether it is just a casual interest or whether you are adventurous enough to check out the locations for yourself."

- LARRY WILSON, Paranormal Investigator/Independent Film Maker

"If you are an investigator or simply an enthusiast, Haunting the Prairie is a must have! Kleen's work is accurate, informative, and makes you rethink the world around you."

- AARON POWERS, F.C.P.S.

This book is dedicated to everyone who has accompanied me on my adventures over the years, and particularly my father for fostering a love for exploration, even if it was only in our backyard.

CONTENTS

INTRODUCTION 1

MAP 7

GUIDE TO SYMBOLS 8

NORTHERN ILLINOIS
Northwestern Illinois 9
Fox River Valley 27
Chicagoland 51

CENTRAL ILLINOIS
The Tract 87
The Heartland 109
East-Central Illinois 133

SOUTHERN ILLINOIS
Metro-East 149
Little Egypt 161

FURTHER READING 188

APPENDIX A
  Articles and News Reports Featuring the Author 193

APPENDIX B
  Illinois Paranormal Research Groups 194

INDEX 198

INDEX BY TOWN AND CITY 202

ABOUT THE AUTHOR 204

Haunting the Illinois | ix

INTRODUCTION

If you are reading this, you are part of a small but dedicated circle that relishes in the exploration of the unknown and unusual. You are a paranormal tourist—someone who goes to cemeteries to admire the scenery, who patronizes bars late at night in the hopes of seeing the lights flicker without explanation, and who risks being fined for trespassing at abandoned buildings. If you are like me, you might even drive an hour and a half to southwest suburban Chicago in the hopes of seeing Resurrection Mary.

The first paranormal tourists in Illinois were the men and women who traveled miles of dirt roads in wagons and on horseback to witness the strange feats of the Williams sisters in Franklin County in 1870, the boys who chased after the Diamond Island Phantom in 1885, or those who picnicked along a road southwest of Macomb in 1908 in the hopes of catching a glimpse of the Gooseneck Ghost.

For someone interested in visiting the mysterious places of Illinois, however, there is no better moment than now to be young, independent, and have a lot of free time in which to travel. You see, most of the resources available to you today did not exist in even the recent past. When I first began exploring Illinois in 1998, I still had a dial-up Internet connection and AOL 3.0. The only way to locate a rural cemetery was to visit the local genealogical society, call a funeral home, or ask a gas station attendant. Most small-town ghost stories never saw the light of day, unless you heard about them on a tour or read about them in a book. Unfortunately, in the mid-1990s, there were less than a half dozen books on haunted places anywhere in Illinois.

1800s – Between the late 1860s and 1880s, the *Chicago Daily Tribune* publishes reports of a sea serpent in Lake Michigan, while newspapers like the Decatur *Daily Republican* churn out stories of encounters with small town ghosts all over Illinois.

1930s – Professors Harry Middleton Hyatt and Charles Neely collect folklore and ghost stories from around Adams County and Southern Illinois.

1950s – John W. Allen writes a weekly column called "It Happened in Southern Illinois," culminating in the 1963 book *Legends & Lore of Southern Illinois*.

1970s – In 1973, Richard T. Crowe begins the first supernatural-themed bus tour in Chicago.

Haunting the Illinois | 1

If you were a child of the 1960s and '70s, your options were even more diminished. Until Beth Scott and Michael Norman wrote *Haunted Heartland* (1985), Illinois ghost stories resided in the pages of local newspapers, esoteric magazines, or academic texts like *Legends & Lore of Southern Illinois* (1963), *Folk-lore from Adams County, Illinois* (1935), and *Tales and Songs of Southern Illinois* (1938). The only way to find your favorite mystery spot was to accompany an older sibling or classmate, who had heard about it from a friend, who heard someone whisper about it in the hallway at school. There was no GPS or Google. Instead, you had to unfold and decipher impractically-large paper maps while trying not to drive off the road. Refolding them was like attempting to solve a Rubik's Cube.

When I was a child, I gobbled up every book I could get my hands on related to ghost stories and the paranormal. *World's Most Spine-Tingling "True" Ghost Stories*, *World's Weirdest "True" Ghost Stories*, and of course, *Scary Stories to Tell in the Dark*, were all favorites. Every week, I eagerly waited for *Unsolved Mysteries* to come on, hoping that night's episode would feature a haunted place. My first real taste of local ghostlore came in April 1991, when my father took a friend and I to see Richard T. Crowe speak at Oakton Community College in Des Plaines. I was in high school when Ursula Bielski's *Chicago Haunts* came out. In my humble opinion, I still consider this to be the best book written about ghostlore in Illinois in the past twelve years. I remember renting it from the library and picking Bachelor's Grove Cemetery as the place I wanted to visit the most. As comprehensive and well researched as *Chicago Haunts* was, however, specific directions were not a strong point. Directions were never a strong point in ghost literature at the time

---

1970s (cont.) – Brad Steiger publishes *Psychic City: Chicago* (1976). In 1977, Martin Riccardo founds the Ghost Trackers Club, later known as the Ghost Research Society. James Shelby Downard (aka Jim Brandon) includes Bachelor's Grove in his book *Weird America* (1978).

1980s – Jan Harold Brunvand publishes The *Vanishing Hitchhiker* (1981). In 1982, Dale Kaczmarek takes over ownership of the Ghost Research Society. *Ghostbusters* (1984) makes every adolescent boy want to own a PKE Meter. Beth Scott and Michael Norman publish *Haunted Heartland* (1985), featuring two dozen ghost stories from Illinois.

1990-1995 – Journalist Kenan Heise publishes his novel *Resurrection Mary: A Ghost Story* (1990).

because the places discussed were meant to be enjoyed from your living room or in the safe company of a professional tour guide.

Nevertheless, my stubborn sense of adventure led my friends and I to continue searching until we found the legendary cemetery, and it took three trips to Midlothian and three afternoons of being bitten by mosquitoes while trudging through forest preserves to do it. After that, I was hooked. When I attended Eastern Illinois University in Charleston, I sought out all the information I could find on haunted places in the area. Being in central Illinois naturally led me to Troy Taylor's books, but other than Pemberton Hall's resident ghost (which Beth Scott and Michael Norman first wrote about in *Haunted Heartland*), Coles County was virgin territory. Charleston, Mattoon, and Ashmore—the three principal towns in the county—briefly received mention in the Shadowlands *Index of Haunted Places*. The dusty archives of the *Daily Eastern News* yielded more information. Unlike other university newspapers, the *Daily Eastern News* never took itself too seriously, at least not enough to dismiss articles about ghost stories.

On Thursday, October 3, 2002, Troy Taylor came and spoke at Eastern Illinois University. Much younger, more naive, and more ignorant of the "eccentricities" of this subculture than I am today, I was dutifully star-struck. I wrote in my journal, "Wherever anyone would have some doubts about the legitimacy of a story he also expressed doubts. He never jumped to any hasty conclusions, he had a very open mind, and even added a dose of sarcasm to his stories." As I recall, the event was fairly well attended, demonstrating a healthy enthusiasm for the subject among my peers.

As far as Illinois is concerned, Richard Crowe, Dale Kaczmarek, Ursula

1990-1995 (cont.)
– In April 1991, 9-year-old Michael Kleen attends a talk by Richard T. Crowe at Oakton Community College. On February 9, 1994, Resurrection Mary is featured in an episode of *Unsolved Mysteries*. www.theshadowlands.net goes online December 1994. Troy Taylor publishes *Haunted Decatur* (1995).

1996-2000 – In August 1996, Matt Hucke launches www.graveyards.com. Ursula Bielski publishes *Chicago Haunts* (1997). Troy Taylor writes a dozen books on the ghostlore of Illinois and the United States, including *The Ghost Hunter's Handbook* (1997). In 1998, www.theshadowlands.net begins compiling a list of haunted places in all 50 states. Scott Markus and Mary Czerwinski film the documentary *Voices from the Chicago Grave* (2000).

Bielski, and Troy Taylor make up the "big four" of the older generation of paranormal researchers. The new generation is much more tech savvy, impetuous, and less likely to be interested in cults of personality. Blogs and social networking sites have replaced the AOL or Angelfire homepage along with their animated skulls and .MIDIs of the Exorcist theme. Digital Cable television, with its hundreds of channels for every conceivable interest, has also revolutionized the way our generation looks at the paranormal. For better or worse, shows such as *Ghost Hunters* and *Paranormal State* have created a paradigm of investigative teams with clever acronyms who are passionate about using technology to determine the truth or falsehood of paranormal events. Granted, there were a few paranormal researchers and research groups before, but the sheer number of them ballooned after *Ghost Hunters* premiered in 2004.

In 2004, I chose to go a different way. Still at EIU, I organized an informal group that met every September and October to travel to haunted places around Coles County and share our common interest in the paranormal. We talked about our own experiences, toured the local sites, played games, and watched horror movies. One year we even told ghost stories around a campfire. The purpose of these activities was to reconnect with all the various ways we enjoy the unusual side of life, much of which has taken a backseat to gadgetry, liability waivers, and competing egos. Let's not forget the reason we walk the line between the real and unreal, between life and the possibility of an afterlife: because it's fun.

In my mind, there is a world of difference between scientific or pseudoscientific research into the paranormal and the act of collecting and retelling folklore and ghost stories. Unfortunately, the distinction between the two has often been blurred. I have received many e-mails from ghost hunting groups claiming to have "debunked" the ghost stories at certain locations, not understanding that a ghost story is

---

2001-2005 – In 2001, Jason Snider forms the Crawford County Ghost Hunters. Michael Kleen begins researching the folklore of Coles County and publishes *Tales of Coles County, Illinois* (2004). In 2004, Dale Kaczmarek founds Ghost Research Society Press and Dan Jungles forms the Will County Ghost Hunters Society. William Gorman researches ghost lore around Rockford and publishes *Ghost Whispers* (2005), and John Kachuba publishes *Ghosthunting Illinois* (2005).

different from a paranormal event and isn't true or false in the way that a fact is either true or false. You can conduct tests to determine if the cold spot in a room was caused by an open window, for example, but you can't conduct tests to determine if your cousin really saw a headless horseman three years ago. In all honesty she probably didn't, but the ambiguity, imagination, and play involved is what makes these stories enjoyable.

The thrill of discovery, danger, and the unknown is what keeps us coming back, whether you are a researcher or a tourist. I know I'll never forget the time I accidentally drove into a cornfield during one nighttime, fog-shrouded trip to Airtight Bridge in rural Coles County. In addition to my many wonderful memories, being at EIU opened up many opportunities, especially when Scott and Tanya Kelley bought Ashmore Estates. Ashmore Estates was the former county poor farm and had served as a psychiatric facility for a number of years before it closed in the 1980s. Like so many of those places, when the patients and staff move out, ghost stories moved in. In 2006, when Scott and Tanya converted the building into a haunted house, I had no idea my research into that place would land me in documentaries and give me speaking opportunities.

For me, the stories were one thing, but I wanted to learn everything I could about the building. It wasn't easy. I spent hours in front of the microfilm reader scanning past issues of the *Times-Courier*. The chapter on Ashmore Estates in my book *Paranormal Illinois* is the culmination of years of research, and I recommend it to everyone.

I created the *Legends and Lore of Illinois* digital newsletter in 2007 in order to be challenging, creative, entertaining, and informative at the same time. I wanted to provide the background information backed up with research that I felt was so lacking in a lot of previous books on Illinois ghostlore. Furthermore, I wanted to apply the methods I learned at the graduate level as a history student at EIU. The introduction of citations in my book *Paranormal Illinois* was one way

2006-Present – February 2006, Willy Adkins forms the Illinois Ghost Hunters. Michael Kleen publishes the monthly e-serial *Legends and Lore of Coles County* (2006) and *Legends and Lore of Illinois* (Jan. 2007-2010). In 2007, the first Chicago Ghost Conference is held and Chad Lewis and Terry Fisk publish *The Illinois Road Guide to Haunted Locations*. In 2010, A&E Network premiers *Paranormal Cops*, featuring the Chicago Paranormal Detectives.

Haunting the Illinois | 5

of achieving this goal. Looking at the subject from a historiographic perspective was another. It's amazing what you discover when you compare what three or four authors have written about one particular story. This book, *Haunting Illinois,* is meant to get you started as someone who just wants to visit these places for fun, or someone who wants to do more in-depth research.

This book is, first and foremost, about our history, our stories, and our shared experiences with the strange and unusual that makes this state unique. If you wish to read more about my adventures over the years, however, I've provided an appendix with a list going back to 2004 of all the newspaper articles in which I've appeared. I honestly hope that you visit the places listed in this book, and always remember, the point is to have fun, get scared, and learn something along the way.

If you plan to visit any of the locations in this book, please be respectful and only visit during hours in which they are open to the public. Take only pictures, leave only footprints. For more information about haunted places in Illinois, plus interviews, articles, top 10 lists and more, visit www.trueillinoishaunts.com. Happy hunting!

♦ ♦ ♦

Haunting the Illinois | 7

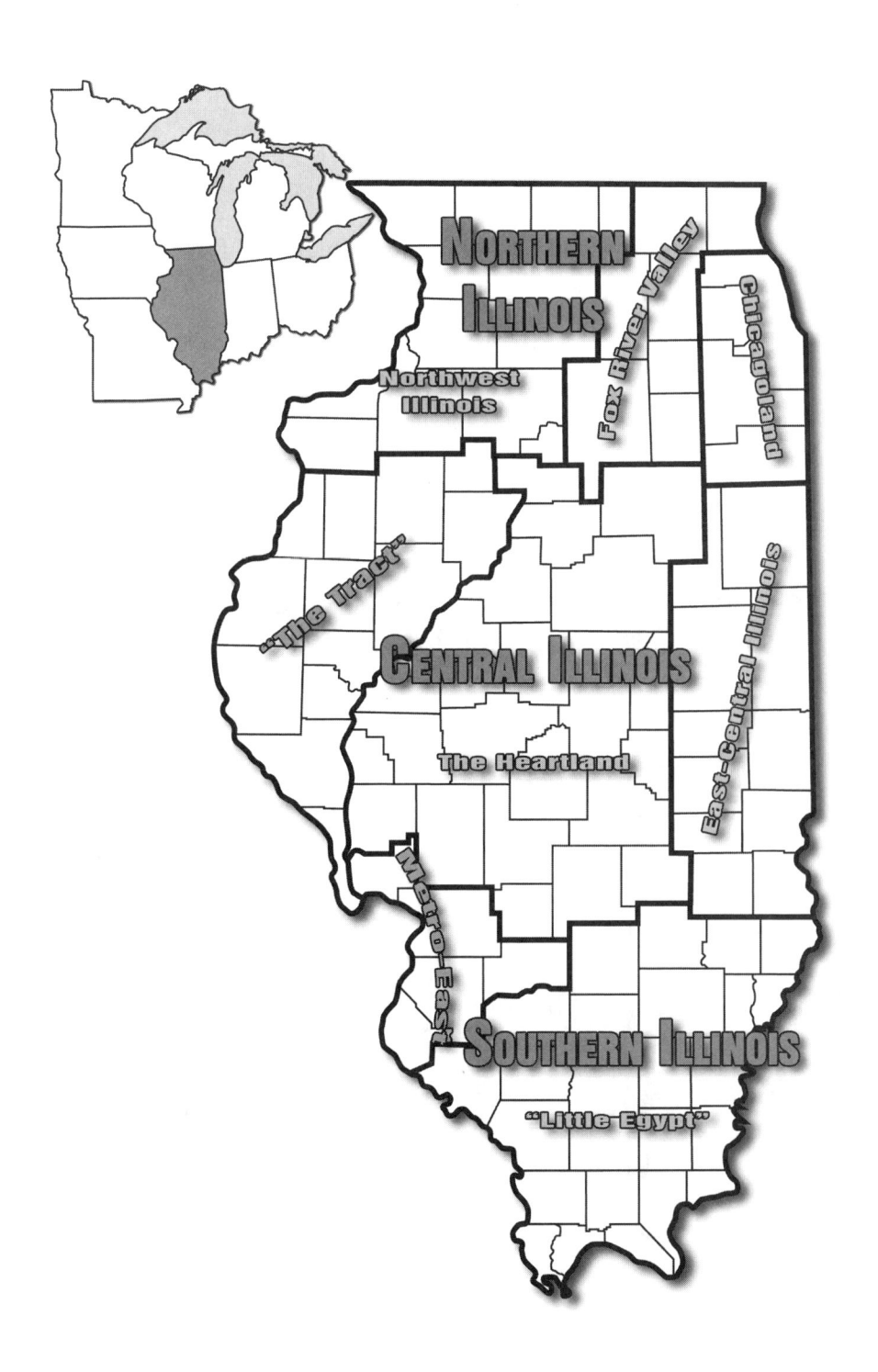

GUIDE TO SYMBOLS

"CREEP FACTOR"

👻 = Unusual but not haunted, or defunct.

👻👻 = A local story. Somewhat active or most likely an urban legend.

👻👻👻 = Sightings occur regularly, involve more than 2 different ghosts, and has been active for several decades.

👻👻👻👻 = Legendary. Highly active, involves a number of closely-related haunted sites, or is widely known.

Symbol	Meaning	Symbol	Meaning
🏚️	Building	🔪	Murder (Rumored/Real)
🪦	Cemetery	⛤	Occult Activity
	Defunct	P	Patrolled by Police
🔥	Disaster		Road or Railroad
🐾	Fortean Animal		Suicide (Rumored/Real)
👻	Ghost		Treasure
☠️	Hazard		Wilderness

Northwestern Illinois

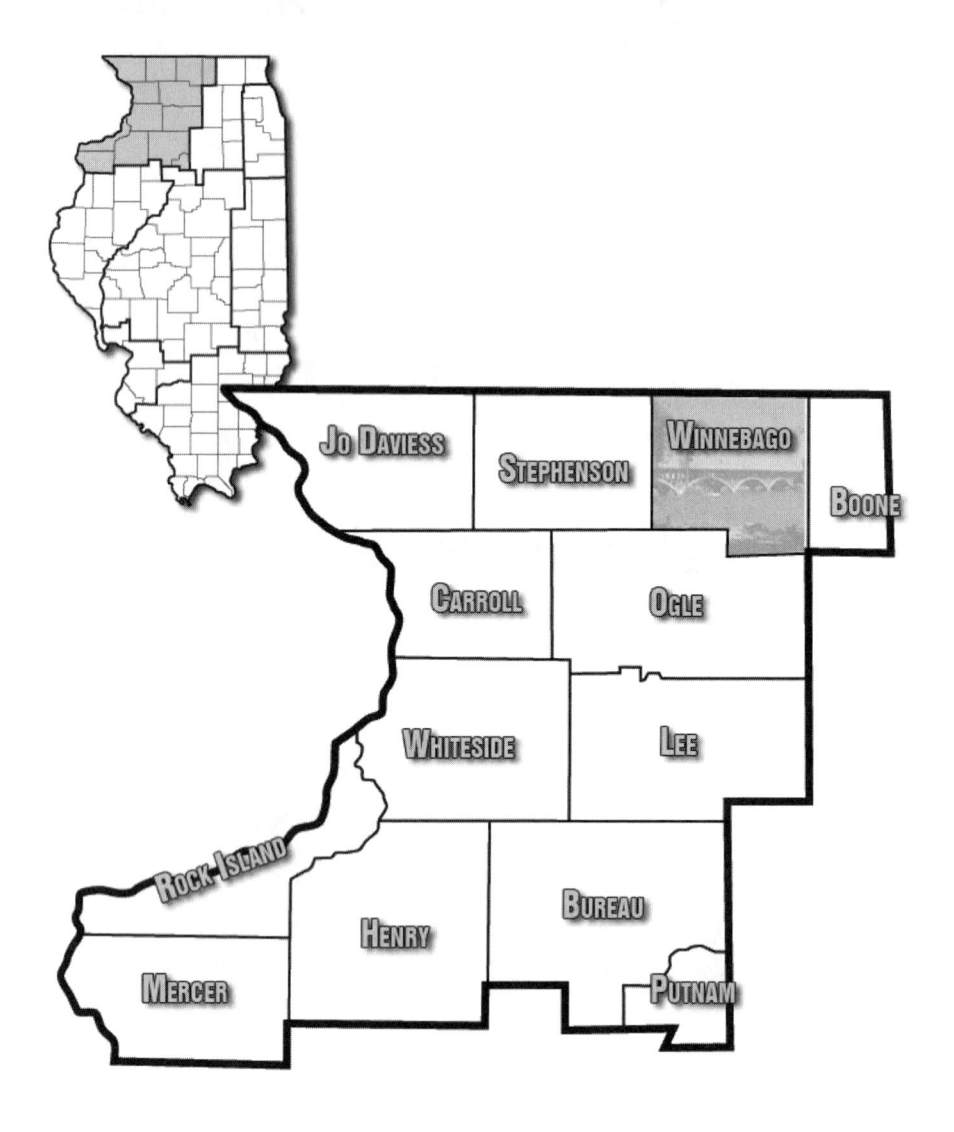

Northwestern Illinois is a very diverse region of the state. Anchored by the metropolitan areas of Rockford and the Quad Cities, this area varies widely in its settlement. For example, the population density of Winnebago County (home of the City of Rockford) is more than 542 people per square mile, while the population density of Henry County is a meager 62 people per square mile. Two of Illinois' six nuclear power plants are located in this region. Prominent waterways include the Mississippi and Rock rivers. Historically, the corridor from Chicago to Rockford and Galena (at the NW tip of Jo Daviess County) was an important trade route. Northwestern Illinois was heavily settled by ethnic Germans and was a Republican stronghold during the Civil War.

10 | *Michael Kleen*

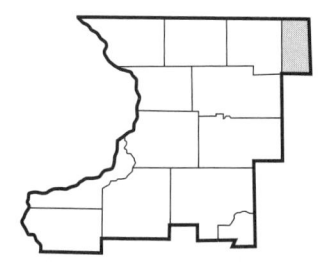

BOONE COUNTY

Population: 41,786
County Seat: Belvidere
Total Area: 282 square miles
Per capita income: $21,590
Year Established: 1837

BELVIDERE

Nellie Dunton Home

A broken-hearted woman is said to haunt this home overlooking the Kishwaukee River. Nellie grew up in Belvidere prior to the Civil War and fell in love with an older man, who promised to marry her after the war. When he failed to return, Nellie refused to fall in love again. She spent the rest of her life in this house. Eventually, she wandered into the river and drowned, some say while wearing her old wedding dress. Her ghost has been seen by residents of this home, as well as by its neighbors.

Source: Gorman, William. *Ghost Whispers: Tales from Haunted Midway*. Rockford: Helm Publishing, 2005.

The Nellie Dunton home is located at 401 E. Lincoln Ave near the intersection of Lincoln and Webber. This is a private residence.

Flora Township

Blood's Point Road and Cemetery

A cornucopia of urban legends have attached themselves to this aptly-named rural avenue and its neighboring cemetery. Visitors have reported seeing phantom vehicles and a dog with glowing red eyes. According to legend, the railroad bridge was the scene of a deadly school bus accident, as well as more than one hanging. These hangings have also been attributed to a bridge along nearby Sweeny Road. The cemetery itself is said to be visited by a wide variety of phenomenon—from orbs, to a phantom dog, to a vanishing barn, to the disembodied laughter of children and electrical malfunctions. Blood's Point was named after Arthur Blood, the first white settler of Flora Township. Some locals maintain that he brought a curse with him that remains to this day.

Source: Gorman, William. *Ghost Whispers: Tales from Haunted Midway*. Rockford: Helm Publishing, 2005; Kleen, Michael. "Blood's Point Road." *Legends and Lore of Illinois* 2 (September 2008): 1-7.

Blood's Point Road is located southwest of Belvidere in rural Boone County. The cemetery is located at the intersection of Blood's Point and Pearl Street.

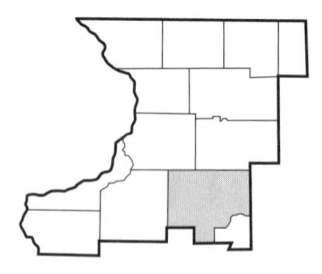

Bureau County

Population: 35,503
County Seat: Princeton
Total Area: 873 square miles
Per capita income: $19,542
Year Established: 1837

CHERRY

1909 Cherry Mine Disaster

The 1909 Cherry Mine fire was the third worst mine disaster in United States history, claiming 259 lives. The fire started on November 13, when kerosene from a lantern dripped into a cart full of hay left for the mules that were used to pull coal cars out of the mine. The fire quickly spread, overwhelming the fan house and the escape ladders, trapping many of the miners inside. Nearly two dozen men survived the fire by sealing themselves behind a wall deep in the mine, where they waited for eight days until the fire subsided and the poisonous gasses disbursed. After the disaster, the Illinois legislature established strict mine safety guidelines.

Source: Tintori, Karen. *Trapped: The 1909 Cherry Mine Disaster*. New York: Atria Publishing, 2002.

The Cherry Mine Disaster memorial is located in Village Park on the north side of Cherry at the intersection of Main and North streets.

SPRING VALLEY

"Help Me" Road

A local legend maintains that in the 1980s a couple was returning home along this road from a night of drinking at a nearby biker bar when their motorcycle crashed. Both riders were terribly injured, but the man managed to write "help me" on the road in his own blood before he died. Attempts to remove the words from the pavement failed. Even when the county repaved the road, the words mysteriously returned. Some have suggested that "help me" was written onto the road in tar by a mischievous construction worker. The road has recently been repaved, and the words are no longer visible—for now.

Haunting Illinois: Northwestern Illinois

Source: http://ghosttraveller.com/spring_valley_il.htm.

"Help Me" Road is located west of Spring Valley along County Road 2775 E, past the pub at the junction of 2775 E and Route 29.

Massock Mausoleum

The Massock Mausoleum in tiny Lithuanian Liberty Cemetery has long been the focus of local curiosity. Visitors have brought back stories of a "hatchet man" that guards the graveyard. The mausoleum itself is said to be warm to the touch and the scene of animal sacrifice. Red paint is spattered on the door, which has been sealed with concrete ever since the late 1960s when two vandals stole a skull from one of the Massock brothers. The Massock brothers' mansion was located in the woods nearby but was torn down in the late 1980s. Local teenagers used to refer to it as the "Hatchet Man's House."

Rosemary Ellen Guiley, in her book *The Complete Vampire Companion*, related the story of several men who encountered a "gaunt, pale figure," in the cemetery at night. Fearing for their lives, they shot at the figure and ran. Later, a reporter who had heard about the men's strange encounter came to the cemetery and poured holy water into a vent in the mausoleum, which produced a groaning sound. Because of the attention this location receives, police routinely patrol the area.

Source: Guiley, Rosemary Ellen. *The Complete Vampire Companion*. New York: Macmillan, 1994; http://ghosttraveller.com /spring_valley_il.htm.

Lithuanian Liberty Cemetery is located northeast of Spring Valley along Peru-Princeton Road, just west of the intersection of 3450 E and Peru-Princeton Road (1350 N).

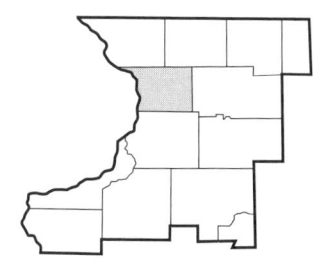

Carroll County

Population: 16,674
County Seat: Mount Carroll
Total Area: 466 square miles
Per capita income: $18,688
Year Established: 1839

Shannon

Willow Creek Farm

Willow Creek Farm dates back to 1838. William Boardman and his wife Mary came from England in 1835 and made their way to Rockford when the future city was merely a trading post. After a few years, William staked out a claim in Cherry Grove Township, Carroll County and erected a log cabin there. According to public records, the current farmhouse dates back to 1878, although there is evidence to suggest it was built more than a decade earlier.

In 2006, Albert Kelchner, the farm's current owner, bought the property and immediately sensed that he was sharing his house with some invisible guests. He began to record his encounters and has invited mediums and paranormal investigators to his farm in the hopes of corroborating his experiences. Home to as many as seven identified ghosts and as many as a dozen others, Willow Creek Farm has been called one of the most active haunted sites in Illinois.

Source: Kleen, Michael. "Willow Creek Farm." *Legends and Lore of Illinois 4* (February 2010): 1-7.

Willow Creek Farm is located at 25516 Spring Valley Road outside of Shannon, Illinois, west of Lake Carroll and Route 73. This is a private residence.

Haunting Illinois: Northwestern Illinois | 15

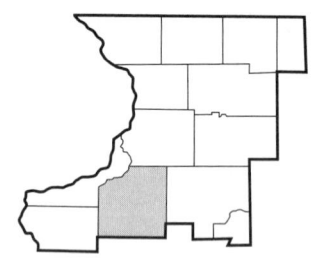

Henry County

Population: 51,020
County Seat: Cambridge
Land Area: 826 square miles
Per capita income: $18,716
Year Established: 1826

Cambridge

"Death Curve"

On the morning of Saturday, September 30, 1905, while her husband labored in a neighboring field, Julia Markham took an ax and murdered her seven children, who ranged from five months to eight years old. Julia had carefully planned the massacre and intended to commit suicide afterward, but the knife that she used to cut her throat was too dull. Reeling from the wound, she laid her children out on a bed, side by side, and doused them with coal oil. She lit the oil on fire and the entire house went up in flames. She intended to die with her children, but the heat of the conflagration proved to be too much and she tried to crawl to safety.

Julia expired soon after rescuers arrived and discovered her grisly crime. Decades passed, and the ruin of the Markham's home was plowed over. Their aging, red barn remained, however, and became a hangout for area youths. Even after the barn was torn down, passersby reported seeing a white specter along the roadside. Locals say that Julia's ghost haunts this curve, tormented by remorse over the murders.

Source: Kleen, Michael. *Paranormal Illinois*. Atglen: Schiffer Publishing, 2010; Lewis, Chad and Terry Fisk. *The Illinois Road Guide to Haunted Locations*. Eau Claire: Unexplained Research Publishing, 2007.

The "Death Curve" is located southwest of Cambridge along Timber Ridge Road. Julia and her children are buried in an unmarked grave in nearby Rose Dale Cemetery.

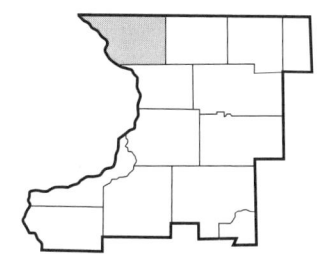

Jo Daviess County

Population: 22,289
County Seat: Galena
Total Area: 619 square miles
Per capita income: $21,497
Year Established: 1827

Galena

Galena History Museum

Daniel Barrows, a wealthy entrepreneur, built this mansion in 1858. The building served as an Odd Fellows Lodge from 1922 to 1938 when it became home to City Hall. The Galena Historical Society took over in 1967. After a few decades, the staff began to notice unusual sounds and kept a log of the occurrences. These experiences included hearing footsteps and banging on the stairs and in the hallways, furniture moving, and even piano keys playing. In 1991, during a wine tasting hosted by the historical society, glasses filled with champagne inexplicably toppled over throughout the evening. One visitor reported seeing a "strangely dressed man," who vanished as mysteriously as he had arrived.

Source: Watson, Daryl. *Ghosts of Galena*. Galena: Galena/Jo Daviess County Historical Society, 1995. Reprint, Dubuque: Welu Printing Company, 2005.

The Galena History Museum is located at 211 S. Bench Street in Galena. It keeps regular hours and tours are conducted during the day.

Horseshoe Mound

In 1907, the *Galena Weekly Gazette* reported that a phantom holding a lantern had been seen nightly moving slowly from Horseshoe Mound to Shot Tower Hill. The ghost was said to be that of a man who had died in a train collision some years before. In modern times, a driver witnessed a "smoky-gray" apparition as he rounded the bend in his car. It hovered just above his windshield before disappearing.

Source: Watson, Daryl. *Ghosts of Galena*. Galena: Galena/Jo Daviess County Historical Society, 1995. Reprint, Dubuque: Welu Printing Company, 2005.

Horseshoe Mound is located east of Galena.
It can be recognized as a sharp, forested bend in Route 20 just outside of town.

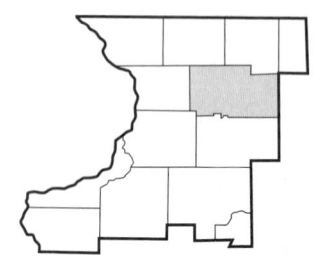

OGLE COUNTY

Population: 51,032
County Seat: Oregon
Total Area: 763 square miles
Per capita income: $20,515
Year Established: 1836

BYRON

Kennedy Hill Road

Between mid-December and early January 1980/81, dozens of people reported seeing a young woman in various stages of dress walking down Kennedy Hill Road outside of Byron. By January 20, 1981, the sightings had reached a fevered pitch. Motorists parked their cars in the frigid temperatures along the narrow rural road to catch a glimpse of what became known as "The Phantom Lady of Kennedy Hill Road." Newspaper reports reached as far away as Chicago, and the Rockford *Register Star* ran five consecutive articles on the sightings.

Explanations for the phantom varied from the ghost of a woman who had been buried in a nearby cemetery, to a mentally disabled girl who ran away from home, to even a transvestite who wore his girlfriend's clothes after she died in an accident. The phantom disappeared after the snow thawed that spring and was never seen again.

18 | *Michael Kleen*

Source: Kaczmarek, Dale. *Windy City Ghosts: An Essential Guide to the Haunted History of Chicago*. Oak Lawn: Ghost Research Society Press, 2005; Kleen, Michael. *Paranormal Illinois*. Atglen: Schiffer Publishing, 2010; Rowe, Bill. "Was Byron's Barefoot Phantom Merely a Masquerade?" *Rockford Magazine* 11 (Fall 1996): 24-25.

Kennedy Hill Road is located north of Byron off of Route 2. Most of the phantom lady sightings occurred near the intersection of Kennedy Hill and Short Road.

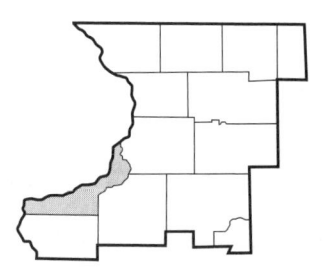

ROCK ISLAND COUNTY

Population: 147,347
County Seat: Rock Island
Total Area: 451 square miles
Per capita income: $20,164
Year Established: 1831

MOLINE

"Pointing Ghost" of 23rd Avenue

Seen less frequently in recent years, the "Pointing Ghost" is an anonymous phantom woman who appears in Victorian garb along 23rd Avenue in Moline. She has alternatively been accused of inaccurately predicting deaths and criminal convictions, and of even misdirecting an inebriated man to the balcony rather than the restroom. She is called the "Pointing Ghost" because she is always seen with her arm outstretched, pointing at someone or in some direction.

Source: Carlson, Bruce. *Ghosts of Rock Island County, Illinois*. Fort Madison: Quixote Press, 1987; Lewis, Chad and Terry Fisk. *The Illinois Road Guide to Haunted Locations*. Eau Claire: Unexplained Research Publishing, 2007.

The Pointing Ghost has been seen along 23rd Avenue, which is located west of 16th Street and Whitey's Ice Cream Store in Moline.

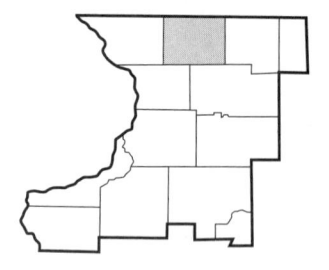

STEPHENSON COUNTY

Population: 48,979
County Seat: Freeport
Total Area: 565 square miles
Per capita income: $19,794
Year Established: 1837

FREEPORT

Guiteau Home

Locally known as the "Saltbox Place," this unassuming stone house is rumored to have been the boyhood home of President James Garfield's assassin, Charles Guiteau. Guiteau possessed delusions of grandeur and believed that he had been personally responsible for Garfield's nomination at the 1880 Republican Convention. After President Garfield denied his application for an ambassadorship to France, Guiteau decided that God had told him to assassinate the president. On July 2, 1881, he shot Garfield twice in the back. For eleven weeks, the president lay in agony, until he finally died due to an infection in September. Guiteau was hanged on June 30, 1882.

Charles Guiteau's remains were never found, and some locals believe that his bones were secreted back to Freeport, where they were buried in the basement of the "Saltbox Place." In fact, neither Charles nor his parents ever owned this house. According to the *Journal-Standard*, that distinction belonged to Guiteau's aunt and uncle. Nevertheless, tenants living in the home after Guiteau's execution reported an oppressive, dark presence and the smell of sulfur. The house is currently being renovated after sitting abandoned for a number of years.

Source: "Myths still persist in Guiteau story," *Journal-Standard* (Freeport) 1 August 2008; Gorman, William. *Ghost Whispers: Tales from Haunted Midway.* Rockford: Helm Publishing, 2005.

The Guiteau House is located at the corner of S. Galena (Business Route 20) and S. High avenues in Freeport. It is currently closed to visitors.

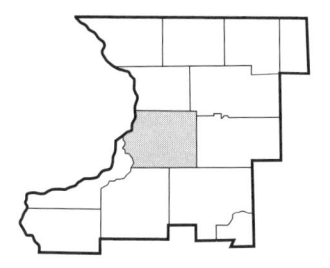

Whiteside County

Population: 60,653
County Seat: Morrison
Total Area: 697 square miles
Per capita income: $19,296
Year Established: 1836

Albany

Albany Mounds

Dating from the Middle Woodland (Hopewell) period, Albany Mounds is the oldest archaeological site in Illinois. It predates both the Cahokia and Dickson Mounds and contains 39 of its original 96 burial sites. While the nearby settlement site is privately owned, visitors can access the Albany Mounds from a picnic area and bike path.

Source: http://www.illinoishistory.gov/hs/albany_mounds.htm

Albany Mounds State Historic Site is located south of Albany off of Route 84.

Sterling

Seventh Avenue Dead End

Just east of downtown Sterling, 7th Avenue ends in front of a railroad track that runs parallel to the Rock River, which divides Sterling and Rock Falls. Several people have drowned or have been hit by a train in the area. Although 7th Avenue is nearly identical to the other nearby side streets, eyewitnesses have reported seeing or hearing the ghost of a woman there. She is said to be searching for her missing child along the riverbank just over the railroad tracks. While no one really knows who this young woman was in life, many locals have heard the story.

Haunting Illinois: Northwestern Illinois

Source: Kleen, Michael. "Seventh Avenue Dead End." *Legends and Lore of Illinois* 4 (January 2010): 1-6; Lewis, Chad and Terry Fisk. *The Illinois Road Guide to Haunted Locations*. Eau Claire: Unexplained Research Publishing, 2007.

To get to the Seventh Avenue Dead End, follow 7th Avenue south from Route 2 until it ends. 7th Avenue should not be confused with 7th Street, which runs east-west.

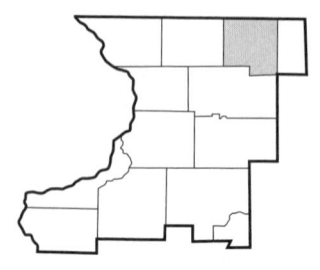

WINNEBAGO COUNTY

Population: 278,418
County Seat: Rockford
Total Area: 519 square miles
Per capita income: $21,194
Year Established: 1836

ROCKFORD

Coronado Theater

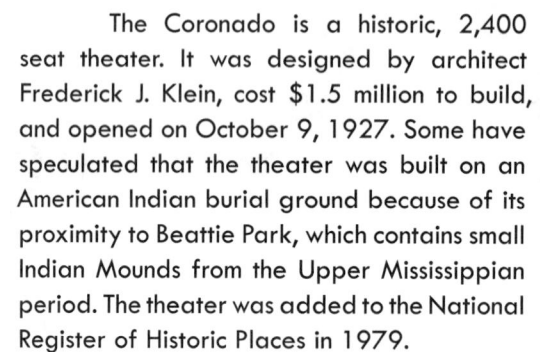

The Coronado is a historic, 2,400 seat theater. It was designed by architect Frederick J. Klein, cost $1.5 million to build, and opened on October 9, 1927. Some have speculated that the theater was built on an American Indian burial ground because of its proximity to Beattie Park, which contains small Indian Mounds from the Upper Mississippian period. The theater was added to the National Register of Historic Places in 1979.

According to a local psychic named Mark Dorsett, three ghosts haunt the theater: Willard Van Matre, the Coronado's original owner who died in 1953; Miss Kileen, the theater's first office manager; and Louis St. Pierre, a Bridge enthusiast and the first theater manager. While Van Matre likes to greet visitors at the theater entrance, the scent of lilac perfume is associated with Miss Kileen. Other people have reported feeling "uneasy" on the catwalks, allegedly because they are occupied by the ghosts of men who died during construction of the building.

Source: "A Haunting in Rockford?" WIFR Channel 23 News (Rockford) 5 May 2009; http://en.wikipedia.org/wiki/Coronado_Theater.

The Coronado Theater is located at 314 North Main Street in Rockford. It is open to the public during regular show times.

Emma Jones Home

Emma Pauline Jones was a Norwegian immigrant who lived at this home (built in 1856) from the 1920s into the 1950s. Her husband Frank was often away on business, and she spent much of her time with her two beloved Dalmatians, Moxie and Channing. After her husband died in 1941, Emma—who was 66 years old—continued to live with her faithful dogs, but after they passed on, she began to descend into loneliness and dementia. She spent her twilight years sitting in a rocking chair, waiting for loved ones who would never return.

Emma finally sold her home and moved in with a relative, where she died in 1964. According to local legend, she returned to her house on North First Street in her afterlife. Owners of the home have reported strange noises, moving furniture, and even seeing the ghost of an elderly woman in the attic windows. One newlywed couple reported that an old woman appeared in their living room and asked what they were doing in her home, then vanished.

Source: Gorman, William. *Ghost Whispers: Tales from Haunted Midway*. Rockford: Helm Publishing, 2005; "Rockford ghost stories live long after their subjects." *Register Star* (Rockford) 30 October 2008.

The Emma Jones home is located in Rockford at the corner of N. 1st and Prairie streets. This is a private residence and is not open to the public.

Rockford College

Rockford College is steeped in history. It was founded in 1847 as Rockford Female Seminary and changed its name in 1892 but remained a predominately female academy until 1958. Jane Addams graduated from the school in 1881. In 1964 the campus was moved from its home along the river to its present location along State Street. Many campus buildings are said to be haunted. The laughter of past students has been heard in the vicinity of Adams Arch, which was constructed using a doorway from the original campus. The ghost of either a student or professor reportedly haunts a former radio station in the Burpee Building. The Clark Arts Center's two theaters are also visited by their own phantoms, one of whom is supposed to be the ghost of the building's architect.

Source: Kleen, Michael. *Paranormal Illinois*. Atglen: Schiffer Publishing, 2010; Taylor, Troy. *Haunted Illinois: The Travel Guide to the History & Hauntings of the Prairie State*. Alton: Whitechapel Productions Press, 2004.

Rockford College is a private college located at 5050 E. State Street, between Alpine and Roxbury roads, in Rockford.

Tinker Swiss Cottage

Built in 1865 on a bluff just south of downtown Rockford, the Tinker Swiss Cottage took its name from its unique architecture, which was inspired by Robert Hall Tinker's visit to Europe in 1862. The Tinker family lived at the home until around 1940, when Mrs. Tinker willed it to the Rockford Park District and it became a museum. In recent years, several paranormal teams instigated the cottage after visitors repeatedly asked the museum curators if it was haunted. During one investigation, a woman's voice appeared on an audio recorder saying, "I don't like trains…

24 | Michael Kleen

trains bring death," as a train passed by on the railroad tracks outside. At other times, doors closed with no apparent explanation.

Source: http://www.tinkercottage.com/the-cottage.htm; http:// tinkercottagemuseum.wordpress.com/2010/02/10/more-paranormal-investigations-at-tinker/.

Tinker Swiss Cottage is located at 411 Kent Street in Rockford, just east of S. Winnebago and north of Morgan Street. www.tinkercottage.com

Twin Sister's Woods

Twin Sister's Woods is located behind Charles Street in Rockford and is part of Twin Sister Hills Park—22.44 acres of recreational land complete with two baseball fields and three sled hills. It is a popular winter destination, but some locals claim this park is home to more sinister guests. The woods, they say, have been the scene of several murders, hangings, and even a drowning. Feelings of dread, disembodied voices, and mysterious figures are just some of the phenomena experienced by visitors.

There is a large willow tree near the entrance to the woods. According to the Shadowlands Index of Haunted Places for Illinois, "If you walk by the willow tree it is said that you have a strange desire to go into the woods. There is an old hanging tree with some odd carvings on it. A little girl is said to be seen walking around." The little girl is the ghost of a child who allegedly drowned in nearby Keith Creek.

Source: Kleen, Michael. "Twin Sister's Woods." *Legends and Lore of Illinois* 3 (October 2009): 1-8; http://theshadowlands.net/places /illinois.htm.

Parking for Twin Sister Hills Park is located at the end of Harney Court west of 27th Street. 27th Street can be accessed off of Charles Street, across from the campus of East High School. Park closes at dusk.

Haunting Illinois: Northwestern Illinois | 25

Fox River Valley

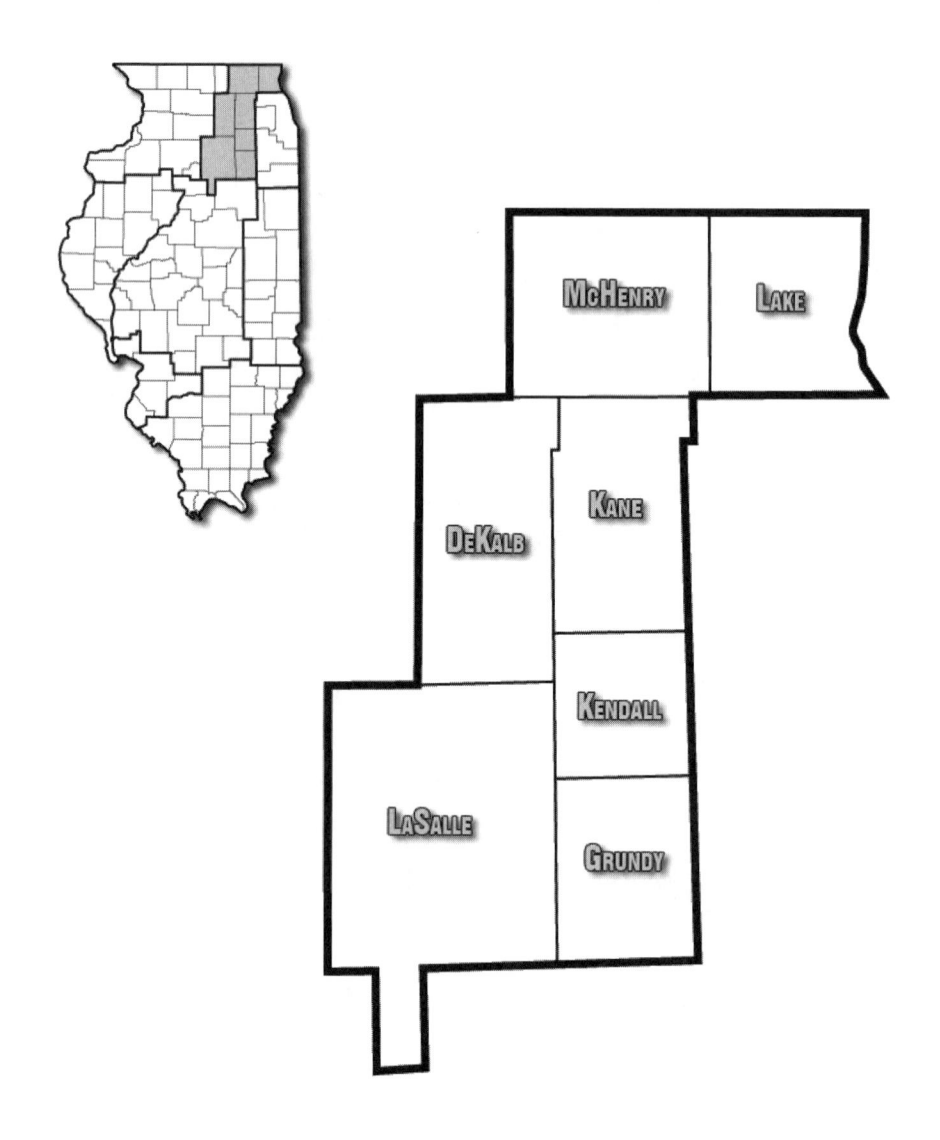

The Fox Valley region is defined by the Fox River, which originates near Menomonee Falls, Wisconsin, and winds its way south to the Illinois River and its tributaries. In northwestern Lake County, the Fox River forms the Chain O'Lakes, which alongside Six Flags Great America makes that area a prime summer vacation spot for Chicagoans. While most counties in the Fox Valley are technically part of the Chicago metropolitan area, this region has a distinct culture rooted in independent, small town life. The Fox Valley also contains some of the wealthiest communities in Illinois.

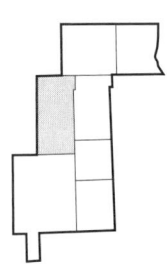

DeKalb County

Population: 88,969
County Seat: Sycamore
Total Area: 635 square miles
Per capita income: $19,462
Year Established: 1837

DeKalb

Egyptian Theater

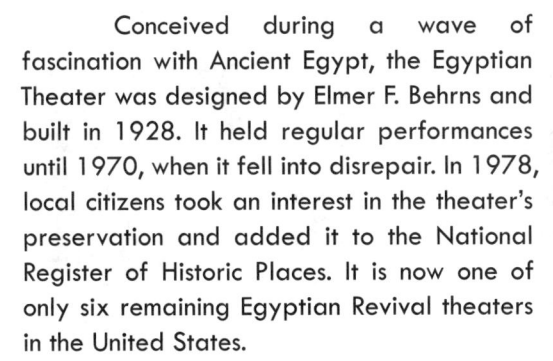

Conceived during a wave of fascination with Ancient Egypt, the Egyptian Theater was designed by Elmer F. Behrns and built in 1928. It held regular performances until 1970, when it fell into disrepair. In 1978, local citizens took an interest in the theater's preservation and added it to the National Register of Historic Places. It is now one of only six remaining Egyptian Revival theaters in the United States.

According to Operations Director Alex Nerad, the theater is haunted by two ghosts: one of Irv Kummerfeldt, whose leadership saved the building in 1978 and who died at the top of Isle 1, and one simply known as "Bob." Open doors, footsteps, and mysterious taps on the shoulders of employees are all blamed on Bob. The Egyptian symbols in the theater have been said to contain hidden messages.

Source: "Survive like an Egyptian," *Northern Star* (DeKalb) 13 October 2006; http://en.wikipedia.org/wiki/Egyptian_Theatre_(DeKalb,_Illinois)

*The Egyptian Theater is located at 135 N. 2nd Street in DeKalb.
It is open to the public during regular show times.*

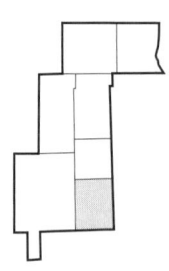

Grundy County

Population: 37,535
County Seat: Morris
Total Area: 430 square miles
Per capita income: $22,591
Year Established: 1841

Minooka

Aux Sable Cemetery

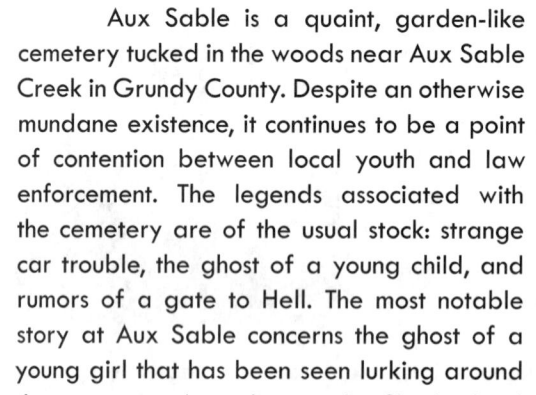

Aux Sable is a quaint, garden-like cemetery tucked in the woods near Aux Sable Creek in Grundy County. Despite an otherwise mundane existence, it continues to be a point of contention between local youth and law enforcement. The legends associated with the cemetery are of the usual stock: strange car trouble, the ghost of a young child, and rumors of a gate to Hell. The most notable story at Aux Sable concerns the ghost of a young girl that has been seen lurking around the cemetery. According to the Shadowlands Index of Haunted Places for Illinois, the ghost will only appear if you get out of your car. Recently, someone removed the headstone of a six year old girl from the cemetery and left it on the playground of an elementary school. The ghost allegedly belongs to this particular girl.

Source: Kleen, Michael. "Aux Sable Cemetery." *Legends and Lore of Illinois* 3 (July 2009): 1-8; http://theshadowlands.net/places/illinois.htm.

Aux Sable Cemetery is located south of Interstate-80 at the end of Brown Road, which can be accessed off E. Minooka Road west of Minooka.

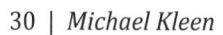

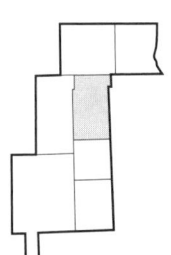

Kane County

Population: 404,119
County Seat: Geneva
Total Area: 524 square miles
Per capita income: $24,315
Year Established: 1836

Elgin

Channing Elementary School

Channing Elementary School has the unfortunate distinction of having been built over what remained of Elgin's first cemetery. During the 1940s, most of the graves were moved to accommodate a new sports field, but in the 1960s, when construction crews broke ground on the new elementary school, their equipment began to uncover human remains. Since then, faculty and staff at Channing Elementary have reported an elevator that seems to move on its own, footsteps on the roof, dark figures, and even scratching on the walls. Today, a stone monument to the dead buried at the original cemetery sits at a nearby park.

Source: Bielski, Ursula. *More Chicago Haunts: Scenes from Myth and Memory.* Chicago: Lake Claremont Press, 2000.

Channing Elementary School is located at 63 South Channing Street in Elgin, just north of Channing Park. The school is not open to the general public.

Haunting Illinois: Fox River Valley | 31

GENEVA

Vere Cory Home

Miss Vere Cory lived in Geneva from 1894 until her death in 1982. She was an accomplished pianist who prided herself on her elegant dress, and she performed recitals all over the United States, even receiving invitations from two U.S. presidents: William Taft and Woodrow Wilson. She toured Europe between world wars. Back in Geneva, she taught piano lessons from her imposing home, in which she lived until her death. Her parlor was said to be lit by only one lamp. After her death, her home was sold and turned into the Kris Kringle Haus. Several years later, the home was moved from Third Street to James Street, where it is now occupied by a sewing shop. Despite the move, Miss Cory's ghost is thought to have remained there, and passersby have heard the sweet melody of a piano echoing from the home.

Source: http://geneva.patch.com/articles/can-you-still-hear-vere-corys-haunting-melody

Vere Cory's home was formerly located on Third Street, but was recently moved to 216 James St. where it is now the Designer Desk Complete Needlework Shoppe. The shop is open during regular business hours.

Fox Run Subdivision

Shortly after construction was completed on the Fox Run Subdivision, some residents began to report eerie encounters. Most of these encounters centered on the tiny cemetery at the southwest end of the subdivision, but some—notably ethereal singing, knocking, and a physically aggressive phantom wearing an old-fashioned suit—were experienced by at least one resident in her

32 | *Michael Kleen*

home. The Fox Run Subdivision had been built over the former site of the Illinois State Training School for Girls, which operated between 1893 and 1978. The purpose of the "school" was to rehabilitate juvenile girls who had been convicted of a crime in the Illinois court system.

Inevitably, deaths from illness and suicide occurred at the facility over the course of its 85 years in operation. Girls without families, or who had been disowned, were buried in a cemetery on the property. Several infants were buried there as well, and today the cemetery contains 51 graves. Since the 1940s, visitors have reported seeing red eyes in the woods around the cemetery, as well as the specter of a woman in a white gown or flowing dress in the cemetery itself. Others have heard a crying infant. The developers of Fox Run agreed to maintain the cemetery in perpetuity, so it will always remain as a reminder of what was once there.

Source: "Cries, Eyes, and Dead Brides," *Kane County Chronicle* (Geneva) 27 October 2008; http://geneva.patch.com/articles/beware-the-girls-school-ghosts; http://geneva.patch.com/articles/girls-school-grave-sites-may-gods-peace-be-with-their-souls

The Fox Run Subdivision is located south of Geneva off Crissey Avenue (Route 25). The girl's school cemetery is located at 764 Fox Run Drive. Cemetery closes at dusk.

North Aurora

Devil's Cave

Waubonsee Indians occupied the land around North Aurora when the first white settlers arrived. According to local legend, one member of the tribe began to steal, so he was banished. He took up living in a nearby cave and covered himself with a fungus that glowed, giving off "foxfire." His people began to believe the cave was occupied by a demon, so they lit a fire and fanned smoke into the entrance. To their surprise, the banished man ran out of the cave and leapt to his death into the Fox River.

Haunting Illinois: Fox River Valley

A slightly more gruesome version of this legend was reported in the *Kane County Chronicle*. This version involved both the Waubonsee and the white settlers. For the most part, the tribe and the settlers got along, but one member of the tribe was not happy and began to play pranks on the settlers. They found out, and he was banished from the village. Over time, some of the settlers were found murdered and scalped. During the search for the perpetrator, they noticed a light coming from a nearby cave in the woods. A joint band of Waubonsee and white settlers lit brush on fire at the entrance to the cave to smoke out whatever was in there. The banished man ran out of the cave, caught fire, and leapt to his death into the Fox River.

Source: The Red Oak Nature Center; "Cries, Eyes, and Dead Brides," *Kane County Chronicle* (Geneva) 27 October 2008.

The Red Oak Nature Center is located off Route 25 at 2343 S. River Street. The park is open year round and trails are open until sunset. www.foxvalleyparkdistrict.org

St. Charles

Al Capone's Hideaway and Steak House

Stories of prohibition-era gangsters are common around Chicago, but it is rare when an establishment can claim a legitimate connection. That is the case for this restaurant along the Fox River, which, during the 1920s, was known as Reitmayer's Beer Garden and was fought over by the likes of Al Capone and Bugs Moran. Its isolated location made it the perfect place for a speakeasy, and relics from those bygone days are still uncovered during renovations. The ghostly activity at the Hideaway primarily centers on one table on the second floor. The place setting at this table frequently appears "messed with," and napkins have fallen on the floor for no apparent reason, while none of the surrounding tables were similarly disturbed. The door between the bar and the dining area also swings back and forth as though someone is walking through it. According to staff, none of this activity has felt threatening.

Source: Crowe, Richard T. *Chicago's Street Guide to the Supernatural*. Oak Park: Carolando Press, 2000, 2001.

Al Capone's Hideaway & Steakhouse is located at 35W337 Riverside Drive in St. Charles and is open during regular business hours.
http://www.al-capone.com/steakhouse/

Dunham-Hunt Home

The Dunham-Hunt home is one of St. Charles' oldest buildings. It was built in the late 1830s and was the first brick home in St. Charles. Today, it is a museum and is listed on the National Register of Historic Places. The home remained in the Hunt family for over a century until it was finally purchased in the 1980s by Jane Dunham to prevent its demolition.

According to Bethany Krajelis of the *Kane County Chronicle*, "Museum stall have reported hearing footsteps, seeing moving shadows under doors, and claw marks on the wallpaper, as well as neighbors reporting flickering lights." One former museum director held a séance in the home. The haunting continues to the present day.

Source: http://www.st-charles.lib.il.us/history/hunt.htm; "A Ghostly Welcome: Dunham-Hunt Museum Reopens and Jane Would be Pleased," *Chicago Tribune* (Chicago) 31 May 1998; "Cries, Eyes, and Dead Brides," *Kane County Chronicle* (Geneva) 27 October 2008.

The Dunham-Hunt Museum is located at 304 Cedar Avenue in St. Charles and is open during regular hours.

Haunting Illinois: Fox River Valley | 35

Hotel Baker

The historic Hotel Baker opened on June 2, 1928, and quickly became the toast of the town. It was called the "honeymoon hotel" for its reputation as a getaway and its beautiful riverfront view and garden. Tragedy was not far behind, however. According to local legend, a chambermaid employed at the hotel drowned herself in the Fox River after her fiancé abandoned her at the altar. Another version claims the maid's lover was also a hotel employee, and he left her after a long and disappointing night of poker. The hotel chambermaids formerly lived on the sixth floor, which was converted into the penthouse suite. Guests on the sixth floor report hearing cries and having their bedding disturbed by unseen hands.

Source: "Cries, Eyes, and Dead Brides," *Kane County Chronicle* (Geneva) 27 October 2008; http://www.stcmuseum.org/historic18.html; http://www.ghosttraveller.com/Illinois.htm.

Hotel Baker is located at 100 West Main Street in St. Charles. It is open during regular business hours. www.hotelbaker.com

St. Charles East High School

St. Charles High School used to be located at the corner of Main Street and Seventh Street in a building which is now home to Thompson Middle School. During the late 1970s, the city saw fit to construct a new high school along Dunham Road. Sometime between 1978 and 2000, when the school split into East and North, a story began to circulate about the ghost of a girl who had been raped and murdered there by a janitor. Allegedly, the freshman girl was attacked while practicing her flute in the band room, and the deranged janitor chopped up her body and stuffed the pieces into various lockers. Band students sometimes claim to see body parts in their lockers, only to have them vanish before their eyes. Others have heard the faint sound of a flute playing while alone in the room. On other occasions, flutes have gone missing or appear to have been played during the night. St. Charles East High School has also gone through a spate of bad luck. In 2001, the school had to be closed for several weeks due to a serious mold problem, and during Homecoming 2009, 972 students called in sick with Swine Flu, although it is unknown how many of them actually had the disease.

Source: http://theshadowlands.net/places/illinois.htm; http://en.wikipedia.org/wiki/St._Charles_East_High_School.

St. Charles East High School is located at 1020 Dunham Road, north of East Main Street (Route 64). The school is not open to the general public.

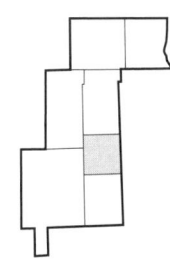

Kendall County

Population: 54,544
County Seat: Yorkville
Total Area: 323 square miles
Per capita income: $25,188
Year Established: 1841

Oswego

Cherry Road

Similar to Spring Valley's "Help Me" Road, Cherry Road outside of Oswego is said to have been the scene of a tragic accident. While predominantly straight, there is a sharp, 90 degree angle toward the end of the road. A young couple allegedly wrecked their car after prom while taking that curve too fast. The boy crawled from the wreckage and wrote "help" in his own blood on the pavement. His girlfriend's ghost can be seen at the bend. Over the years, local teens have painted "Help" on the road with red spray paint.

Haunting Illinois: Fox River Valley

Source: "In search of the valley's ghosts," *Beacon-News* (Aurora) 25 October 2009; "Trail of Fears," *Beacon-News* (Aurora) 30 October 2005.

Cherry Road is located southeast of Oswego between Plainfield Road and Highway 16. The 90 degree angle is located near the intersection with Plainfield Road.

YORKVILLE

Fox Riverfront

Many dams are located near riverfront communities, but the dam in the Fox River near downtown Yorkville has been deemed particularly dangerous. This large, concrete dam was recently rebuilt to include a canoe and kayak chute, but residents remain concerned about the safety of swimmers and boaters in the area. As recently as the summer of 2008, a teenage boy disappeared while swimming in the river with three other friends. According to some local residents, the ghosts of a family who drowned at the Yorkville dam can be seen reenacting their tragedy. The ghosts—a father, mother, and their daughter—walk across the top of the dam in a futile attempt to escape but always vanish before reaching the shore.

Source: "Reactions over Yorkville dam concerns," *Beacon-News* (Aurora) 19 October 2009; http://theshadowlands.net/places/illinois.htm.

The Yorkville dam can be accessed off of E. Hydraulic Street on the south side of the Fox River in Yorkville. Visitors should observe extreme caution, even if there is no water flowing over the surface of the dam.

Yorkville Middle School (Former)

Now home to the Circle Center Grade School, the old Yorkville Middle School is said to be haunted by the ghost of a janitor who died of starvation in 1978 after he was trapped in the school's elevator over summer break. Former students reported feeling as though they were being watched in the hallways even when they were alone. The local newspaper investigated the story and found several inconsistencies, including no record of a death in the building in 1978 and the fact that there is no elevator there.

Source: "In search of the valley's ghosts," *Beacon-News* (Aurora) 25 October 2009.

The former Yorkville Middle School is located at 901 Mill Street in Yorkville. The building is not open to the general public.

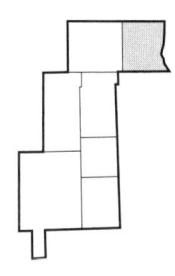

Lake County

Population: 644,356
County Seat: Waukegan
Total Area: 448 square miles
Per capita income: $32,102
Year Established: 1839

Antioch

Antioch Community High School

Antioch Township High School (as it was originally known) has served the community from its campus on Main Street for nearly a century, but progressive renovations and additions have rendered the school unrecognizable from its earliest days. It began as a small rural high school educating under 200 total students. Today, it educates over 2,200 students. Expansions took place in five stages between 1927 and 2002. In 1998, the original buildings were demolished to make room for an administrative office and a media center.

With so much history, it is no wonder Antioch High is rumored to be home to some unusual phenomenon. During the 1990s, about a half dozen former students approached Scott Marcus, author of *Voices from the Chicago Grave*, and informed him of an unusual string of off-campus student deaths during that decade. Additionally, a widespread rumor circulating among alumni was that a drama student had hung himself in the auditorium. In one unnerving incident, an art teacher witnessed the locker doors in a basement hallway swing open in perfect synchronicity. That particular hallway is said to bring chills and discomfort to anyone who is unlucky enough to have a locker there.

Source: Markus, Scott. *Voices from the Chicago Grave: They're Calling. Will You Answer?* Holt: Thunder Bay Press, 2008; http://www.seq uoits.com/about/achs/history/index.html.

Antioch Community High School is located at 1133 Main Street in Antioch. The school is not open to the public. www.sequoits.com

INGLESIDE

Sunnybrook Asylum

In 1905, Jacob Beilhart moved his utopian commune known as the "Spirit Fruit Society" to a 90-acre site along Wooster Lake near the Chain O'Lakes. They valued hard work and free love as a road to salvation. Jacob died in 1908 and the group left after six more years at the farm. During the 1940s and '50s the property was converted into a health spa called Wooster Lake Health Resort. It was soon abandoned. "Urban explorers" took over the site and began to bring back stories about the abandoned camp. It became known as "Sunnybrook Asylum," and visitors speculated that it closed down because the nurses went insane and burned the hospital down—patients and all. In 1995 the camp buildings really did burn down, and the site is currently being developed as a subdivision.

Source: http://lakecountyhistory.blogspot.com/2009/09/beilhart s-spirit-fruit-society.html; Markus, Scott. *Voices from the Chicago Grave: They're Calling. Will You Answer?* Holt: Thunder Bay Press, 2008.

The former "asylum" was located at the end of Sunnybrook Road, but there is now a subdivision at the site and nothing remains of the original buildings.

LAKE FOREST

Barat College (Former)

Originally a Chicago-based academy for young women, Barat College of the Sacred Heart moved to its Lake Forest campus in 1904, where it remained an all-female institution until 1969. During that time, the college was staffed by nuns from the Order of the Sacred Heart.

Over the years, students began to whisper rumors about a janitor's son who allegedly fell to his death in the elevator shaft in Old Main. His ghost was seen in the basement hallway as well as in the art rooms on the third floor. According to author Scott Markus, the boy's ghost has been accused of leaving a blue handprint on student paintings and artwork.

A phantom nun has also been seen through a third floor window. She was said to be connected to a man who committed suicide in the hallway outside her living quarters. Additionally, the scent of flowers permeated the Sacred Heart Chapel, even if no flowers were present. In 2001, DePaul University purchased the college but sold it to a condo developer in 2006. The hall that contained the Sacred Heart Chapel was slated for demolition.

Source: Markus, Scott. *Voices from the Chicago Grave: They're Calling. Will You Answer?* Holt: Thunder Bay Press, 2008; Taylor, Troy. *Haunted Illinois: The Travel Guide to the History & Hauntings of the Prairie State.* Alton: Whitechapel Productions Press, 2004.

The old Barat College campus, most recently the Barat College of DePaul University, is located off Sheridan Road just east of the Metra line in Lake Forest.
www.thebaratfoundation.org

Haunting Illinois: Fox River Valley

Lake Zurich

Cuba Road

Cuba Road sits nestled between the towns of Lake Zurich and Barrington, both upper and upper-middle class retreats. It is the setting of a plethora of paranormal phenomenon, including a phantom car (or cars), a pair of spectral lovers, and a vanishing house. A side street called Rainbow Road formerly had the distinction of being home to an abandoned mansion that some believed was an old asylum. Along Cuba Road sits White Cemetery, which author Scott Markus has referred to as the Bachelor's Grove of the north-Chicago suburbs. This small, rectangular graveyard dates from the 1820s, and its ghostlore concerns mysterious, hovering balls of light.

Source: Crowe, Richard T. *Chicago's Street Guide to the Supernatural*. Oak Park: Carolando Press, 2000, 2001; Kleen, Michael. "Cuba Road." *Legends and Lore of Illinois* 1 (October 2007): 1-6; Markus, Scott. *Voices from the Chicago Grave: They're Calling. Will You Answer?* Holt: Thunder Bay Press, 2008.

Cuba Road runs between Route 12 (Rand Road) and Route 14 (Elmhurst Road) just north of the border with Cook County. White Cemetery is located along Cuba Road just west of Hough Road.

Libertyville

Devil's Gate

According to local legend, sometime in the distant past a private all-girls school stood behind the set of iron gates off of a sharp bend in River Road, deep inside what became the Independence Grove Forest Preserve. One day, a maniac broke into the school and abducted several of the girls. He killed each one and mounted their severed heads on the spikes of the gate. Every full moon, the heads reappear on the rusted spikes.

42 | *Michael Kleen*

In reality, this property, known as the Doddridge Farm, passed through several incarnations as a summer camp. It opened as the Katherine Kreigh Budd Memorial Home for Children in 1926. Between 1936 and the early 1980s, the Catholic archdiocese operated it as St. Francis Boys Camp. The archdiocese then sold the camp to the Forest Preserve, who knocked down all the buildings and converted the nearby gravel pit into a lake. The gate to St. Francis still sits at the entrance to what is now a horse and bike trail.

Source: Kleen, Michael. *Paranormal Illinois*. Atglen: Schiffer Publishing, 2010; Kleen, Michael. "Devil's Gate." *Legends and Lore of Illinois 1* (March 2007): 1-6; Markus, Scott. *Voices from the Chicago Grave: They're Calling. Will You Answer?* Holt: Thunder Bay Press, 2008.

"Devil's Gate" is located at a 90-degree curve in River Road, north of Libertyville. River Road can be accessed off Route 137 (Buckley Road).

WADSWORTH

Mary Worth

Accord to legend, Mary Worth was a notorious witch who lived on a farm west of Gurnee in Lake County in the mid-1800s. Prior to the Civil War, she would capture runaway slaves and torture them in her barn. Outraged locals took the law into their own hands and burned her to death. Some say her bones were buried in St. Patrick's Cemetery, but others say they were buried on her farm. Years later, a house was built over the foundation of the former barn. The family who lived there found a stone on the property and used it as a step beneath their front door. Poltergeist activity quickly followed. In 1986, the house burnt to the ground, and subsequent efforts to build at the location have failed. Some researchers believe this tale is the origin of the "Bloody Mary" urban legend.

Source: Bielski, Ursula. *Chicago Haunts: Ghostlore of the Windy City*. Chicago: Lake Claremont Press, 1998; Brunvand, Jan Harold. *The Mexican pet: More "New"*

Haunting Illinois: Fox River Valley | 43

Urban Legends and Some Old Favorites. New York: W.W. Norton & Company, 1986; Markus, Scott. *Voices from the Chicago Grave: They're Calling. Will You Answer?* Holt: Thunder Bay Press, 2008.

Many believe Mary Worth is buried in Old St. Patrick's Cemetery, which is located on Mill Creek Road, south of Route 173. Cemetery closes at dusk.

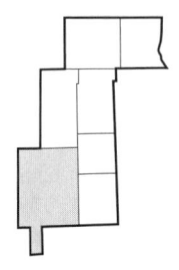

LaSalle County

Population: 111,509
County Seat: Ottawa
Total Area: 1,148 square miles
Per capita income: $19,185
Year Established: 1831

LaSalle

Kaskaskia Hotel

A popular legend maintains that this hotel is haunted by the ghost of a woman who was either murdered or committed suicide there during the 1920s. Chad Lewis and Terry Fisk uncovered a real suicide at the hotel that took place in July 1948. A woman, distraught over her marriage, jumped from the roof and was killed instantly. Employees at the hotel often heard strange footsteps and reported that the elevator would open when no one had pressed the button. The hotel closed in 2001 after changing owners several times but was recently renovated and reopened as a luxury hotel and conference center.

Source: Lewis, Chad and Terry Fisk. *The Illinois Road Guide to Haunted Locations.* Eau Claire: Unexplained Research Publishing, 2007.

The Kaskaskia Hotel is located at 217 Marquette Street in downtown LaSalle.
www.kaskaskiahotel.com

PERU

Saint Bede Academy

St. Bede Academy has a tradition of academic excellence dating back to 1890. For a century, this Benedictine school and abbey has prepared young men and women of the Illinois valley to enter college upon graduation. According to longtime campus legend, there are two eternal residents at the school. "Brother Otto" is the ghost of a monk who is sometimes seen on the third floor. His mortal life ended in a tragic accident, but now he is free to watch over his students for eternity. The second ghost to haunt St. Bede is named "Val." Val was a janitor who stayed in a room above the stage. After his death, his room was used for storage, but his ghost is believed to turn lights on and off, open doors, and move furniture. Students have left a poem for him on the door to his former room, and he is said to protect the auditorium.

Source: http://en.wikipedia.org/wiki/St._Bede_Academy; http:// ghosttraveller.com/Illinois_lasalle_peru.htm.

Saint Bede Academy is located at 24 W. US Highway 6 in Peru and is not open to the general public. www.st-bede.com

UTICA

Starved Rock State Park

Starved Rock State Park is a natural, scenic woodland park surrounding a large butte overlooking the Illinois River. It contains 18 canyons and 13 miles of trails. American Indians inhabited the site for several thousand years before the French arrived and built a fort at the location. According to legend, Potawatomi Indians trapped a group of Illiniwek on the butte and starved them into submission, giving the rock formation its name.

Haunting Illinois: Fox River Valley | 45

In March 1960, three women were murdered in the park, and their bodies were found in one of the canyons. Eventually, a man named Chester Weger was convicted of the crime. Some visitors to the park have claimed to hear groans and other disembodied voices amidst the rock formations.

Between 1685 and 1702, Henri de Tonti was the most powerful man in central Illinois. He accompanied René-Robert Cavelier, Sieur de La Salle in his exploration of the Illinois country, and La Salle left him to hold Fort Saint Louis when he returned to France. During his time in the Illinois River Valley, he is rumored to have accumulated over $100,000 in gold, which he buried around Starved Rock. He told a priest about the gold just before he died, but it has never been found despite search attempts in the 1750s by the French and the Potawatomie.

Source: Henson, Michael Paul. *A Guide to Treasure in Illinois and Indiana*. Dona Ana: Carson Enterprises, 1982; Stout, Steve. *The Starved Rock Murders*. Utica: Utica House Publishing, 1982; Taylor, Troy. *Haunted Illinois: Travel Guide to the History and Hauntings of the Prairie State*. Alton: Whitechapel Productions Press, 2004.

Starved Rock State Park can be accessed off of either Route 178 or Route 71, directly south of the Illinois River and east of Oglesby.

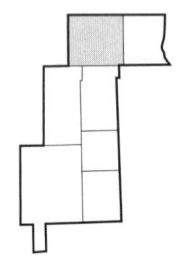

McHenry County

Population: 260,077
County Seat: Woodstock
Total Area: 611 square miles
Per capita income: $26,476
Year Established: 1836

ALGONQUIN

Algonquin Cemetery

Algonquin Cemetery is said to be the home of several nasty spirits that have been "bound" there through occult means. The cemetery is divided by Cary Road into two parts. The more modern, park-like section hasn't attracted the same amount of attention as the older, wooded side, which is said to contain the ghosts of a rapist and a murderer. There is also supposed to be a little boy who warns you when you wander too close to their graves.

Source: http://theshadowlands.net/places/illinois.htm.

Algonquin Cemetery is located at the juncture of Route 31 (Fox River Trail) and Cary Road north of downtown Algonquin on the west side of the Fox River.

CRYSTAL LAKE

Mount Thabor Cemetery

Founded in 1846 by an Irishman who donated an acre of land to the Catholic Church, this cemetery has developed an unusual reputation in McHenry County. According to Dale Kaczmarek, its current compliment of headstones reflect less than a third of its total number of burials. 13 infant graves sit toward the back of the cemetery. All were less than a year of age when they passed away between 1966 and 1968. The temperature is said to noticeably drop in this section. Generally, some visitors to the cemetery have reported seeing a green mist or hearing muttering, singing, and whistling.

Haunting Illinois: Fox River Valley | 47

Source: Kaczmarek, Dale. *Windy City Ghosts II: More tales from America's most haunted city.* Oak Lawn: Ghost Research Society Press, 2005.

Mount Thabor Cemetery is located at the junction of Route 176 and Mt. Thabor Road west of Crystal Lake.

RICHMOND

"King of the Hold Up Men"

Harvey John Bailey (1887–1979) was one of the 1920's most successful bank robbers. He worked in a gang or alone, and his career spanned 13 years and several states. In 1931, his gang robbed the Lincoln National Bank in Lincoln, Nebraska, and made off with roughly $1 million in cash. After the robbery, he is said to have hidden the loot on a farm near Richmond, Illinois, where he had been staying. He robbed his last bank in Kingfisher, Oklahoma, and was sentenced to life in prison on October 7, 1933. He served time until his release in 1964. He died seven years later but without recovering his stash. To this day, no one knows what happened to the $1 million.

Source: Henson, Michael Paul. *A Guide to Treasure in Illinois and Indiana.* Dona Ana: Carson Enterprises, 1982.

Richmond is located less than a mile from the Wisconsin border, at the junction of Route 12 and Route 173.

WOODSTOCK

Woodstock Opera House

This opera house was constructed in 1889 and is as famous for its ghost as it is for its beauty. Its interior was designed to look like a glamorous showboat, and its exterior is an eclectic combination of styles. In the late 1940s, an actor named Shelley Berman witnessed a chair (DD113) that popped up and down during rehearsals, as if someone had been sitting there. After a number of years, the thespians began to refer to their ghost as Elvira. Actresses are warned to stay away from the theater's tower, or else they might feel a strange compulsion to jump. A Honda commercial during the Super Bowl in 1992 even played off the notoriety of the Woodstock's ghost.

Source: Christensen, Jo-Anne. *Ghost Stories of Illinois*. Edmonton: Lone Pine, 2000; Scott, Beth and Michael Norman. *Haunted Heartland: True Ghost Stories from the American Midwest*. New York: Barnes & Noble Books, 1985, 1992.

The Woodstock Opera House is located at 121 West Van Buren Street in downtown Woodstock. It is open during regular show times.
www.woodstockoperahouse.com

Chicagoland

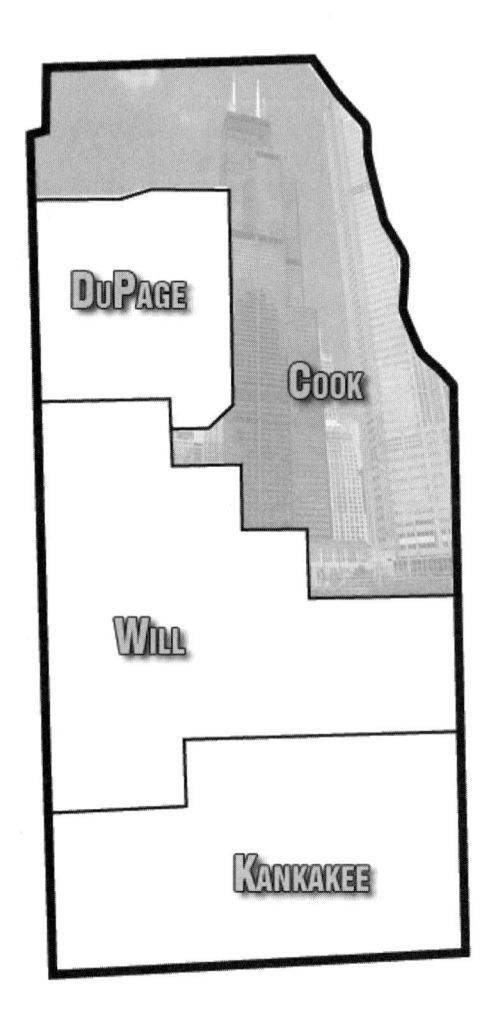

Chicago is the third largest city in the United States and an "alpha city" in the global economy. With 2.8 million people living in the city proper and 8.7 million in its urban fold, it is the political and economic powerhouse of Illinois. With so many people living and dying here (over 2/3 of the state's entire population), it comes as no surprise that the Chicagoland area would be home to so many ghosts. Entire books (and their sequels!) have been devoted to the ghostlore of the Windy City. This section will provide an overview of some of the most interesting or obscure haunted locations.

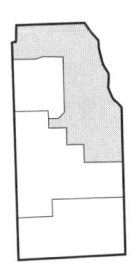

Cook County

Population: 5,294,664
County Seat: Chicago
Total Area: 1,635 square miles
Per capita income: $23,227
Year Established: 1831

Berwyn

Cigars & Stripes

Cigars & Stripes has been a long-time haunt for Berwyn beer and cigar aficionados, but its owner and his customers believe it may also be a haunt of a different kind. According to an article in the *Berwyn/Cicero Gazette* (available on the Cigars & Stripes website), several customers have seen a "shadowy figure" without arms or legs floating down the hallway toward the door leading to the beer garden. Ronn Vrhel, owner of Cigars & Stripes, has heard phantom footsteps on the basement stairs as well. Ronn's wife has also heard shouts and sounds of a party in the basement when no one was present. The ghost of Rose, a former owner of the establishment, is believed to linger in one spot at the bar and play "match maker." She is even credited for bringing together at least one pair of newlyweds. Typical poltergeist activity, such as glasses tipping over and lights turning on and off, has been experienced as well. The paranormal research team Supernatural Occurrence Studies recently investigated the location and walked away convinced that the reported hauntings were real.

Source: "Paranormal Experts Investigate the Haunting of Cigars and Stripes," *Berwyn/Cicero Gazette* (Berwyn) 18 October 2005; http://www.legendsofamerica.com/il-cigars.html.

Cigars and Stripes is located at 6715 West Ogden Avenue in Berwyn, Illinois and is open during regular business hours. www.cigarsandstripes.com

Blue Island

Maple Tree Inn

Ever since Charlie Orr changed the name of Helen's Olde Lantern to Maple Tree Inn, the original owner has not been very happy. The trouble is, Helen Sadunas, who owned the business for nearly 50 years, is dead. Charlie claims that Helen's ghost was stirred up when he bought the restaurant, and he has felt her presence on more than one occasion. His employees have had their own hair-raising experiences. The restaurant's chef felt someone tap him on the shoulder when he was alone in the basement. At Halloween, Charlie transforms the Maple Tree Inn into a haunted house for the enjoyment of his patrons.

Source: Kaczmarek, Dale. *Windy City Ghosts II: More tales from America's most haunted city.* Oak Lawn: Ghost Research Society Press, 2005.

The Maple Tree Inn is located at 13301 S. Old Western Avenue in Blue Island, just south of the Calumet Sag Channel. The Maple Tree Inn is open during regular business hours.

Chicago – Bucktown

Bucktown Pub

The Bucktown Pub is believed to be haunted by a former owner named Wally who committed suicide in 1986. After the bar was purchased from his widow, the new owners made some adjustments to its interior. Much to their surprise, bottles and even coasters and napkins were mysteriously rearranged during the night back to the way they had been when Wally was in charge. The jukebox also turned on and off at will, and employees have reported seeing or hearing someone who vanished when they turned to greet the anonymous visitor.

Source: Crowe, Richard T. *Chicago's Street Guide to the Supernatural*. Oak Park: Carolando Press, 2000, 2001.

The Bucktown Pub is located at 1658 West Cortland Street in Chicago and is open during regular business hours. www.bucktownpub.com.

CHICAGO – CHINA TOWN

Ethyl's Party/Tito's on the Edge

Between 1908 and 1995, Coletta's Funeral Home stood on the edge of China Town and catered to the Italian neighborhood next door. According to Richard T. Crowe, when the funeral home finally moved out and a bar moved in, many locals were weary of patronizing the new establishment. Even one of Tito's own bartenders refused to go into what was formerly the embalming room and the cold storage area in the basement. The building's new owners quickly realized it was haunted. Employees sighted a man dressed in a brown trench coat, a thick white cloud, and even an extra band member who was seen on stage for a few moments before vanishing. Tito's on the Edge is now known as Ethyl's Party, but the strange activity remains.

Source: Bielski, Ursula. *Chicago Haunts 3: Locked Up Stories from an October City*. Holt: Thunder Bay Press, 2009; Crowe, Richard T. *Chicago's Street Guide to the Supernatural*. Oak Park: Carolando Press, 2000, 2001; Markus, Scott. *Voices from the Chicago Grave: They're Calling. Will You Answer?* Holt: Thunder Bay Press, 2008.

Ethyl's Party is located at 2600 South Wentworth Avenue in Chicago and is open during regular business hours.

Haunting Illinois: Chicagoland

Chicago – Dunning

Read-Dunning Memorial Park

Like many poor farms and mental hospitals in Illinois, the Cook County Poor Farm (and the asylum built upon it) had a tragic history. This tragedy spawned a scattering of ghost stories as the modern City of Chicago spread around it and, eventually, over the site itself. The original poor farm, established in 1851, occupied over 150 acres. The Cook County Insane Asylum was built there in 1858 and housed nearly 600 patients by 1885. When much of the complex was finally demolished a century later, the real estate developer who purchased the land was shocked to discover that her construction crews were digging up bodies. Archaeologists conducted an excavation and discovered three cemeteries on the property. The bodies were removed and reburied in a 3-acre park now called Read-Dunning Memorial Park. The Chicago-Read Mental Health Center is also located on land formerly belonging to the poor farm. Residents of the area have told author Ursula Bielski about various ghostly encounters in the stores and other buildings constructed over the original poor farm property, including sightings of the specter of an elderly woman in a hospital gown.

Source: "Mass Grave Found at Construction Site," *Chicago Tribune* (Chicago) 6 May 1989; "Dunning Discovery: Unearthing of Graves on Northwest Side Raises Haunting Questions About Reverence and Neglect," *Chicago Tribune* (Chicago) 9 July 1990; Bielski, Ursula. *Chicago Haunts 3: Locked Up Stories from an October City*. Holt: Thunder Bay Press, 2009.

Read-Dunning Memorial Park is located at the northwest corner of Irving Park Road and Oak Park Avenue, just south of the Chicago-Read Mental Health Center.

Chicago – Edgewater

Ole St. Andrews Inn

During the 1950s, this bar was owned and operated by Frank and Edna Giff. Frank had a legendary taste for vodka, and he had no reservations with sharing a few rounds with his patrons. His lifestyle caught up with him, however, when his wife found him behind the bar, dead at the age of 59.

Edna sold the establishment to a Scot named Jane McDougall, who opened it as the Edinburgh Castle Pub. To Jane's surprise, when she came into work every afternoon she found that her stock of vodka would be measurably lower than when she closed the bar the night before. Employees came and went, but the phenomenon continued. Jane became convinced that no living person was responsible for depleting her vodka. She believed that Frank Giff, along with his taste for his favorite drink, had returned from the grave. When the Edinburgh Castle became the Ole Saint Andrews Inn, poltergeist activity continued. Patrons often felt cold spots, and women in particular felt unseen hands touching their hair and shoulders.

Source: Crowe, Richard T. *Chicago's Street Guide to the Supernatural*. Oak Park: Carolando Press, 2000, 2001; Markus, Scott. *Voices from the Chicago Grave: They're Calling. Will You Answer?* Holt: Thunder Bay Press, 2008.

The Saint Andrew's Inn is located at 5938 N. Broadway Street in Chicago and is open during regular business hours. www.standrewsinnchicago.com.

CHICAGO – HUMBOLDT PARK

Our Lady of Angels School Fire

Our Lady of Angels was a Catholic elementary school serving a predominantly Italian-American neighborhood on the West Side of Chicago. It was a large institution with around 1,600 students. On December 1, 1958, a fire ravaged the school killing 92 students and three nuns, and injuring over 100. It was the third worst school disaster in American history. While the exterior of the school was brick, its interior was mainly wood, and its floors were coated in a flammable wax. The fire began in a basement trash bin, and it went unnoticed for a critical period of time because smoke detectors had not yet become commercially available.

Once the nuns of Our Lady of Angels were alerted to the danger, however, they worked heroically to save their students. Many were trapped and forced to leap from the windows to escape the smoke and flames. Forty-two victims of the fire were interred in Queen of Heaven Cemetery in Hillside, and a monument was erected there called the "Shrine of the Holy Innocents." Survivors of the disaster have worked hard to preserve the memory of the fire and the legacy of its victims.

Source: "Remembering Our Lady of Angels: Gathering Recalls Deadly '58 Fire," *Chicago Tribune* (Chicago) 2 December 2003; Cowan, David. *To Sleep with the Angels: The Story of a Fire*. Chicago: Ivan R. Dee, 1996; McBride, Michele. *The Fire That Will Not Die*. Palm Springs: ETC Publications, 1979.

Our Lady of Angels was formerly located at 909 N. Avers Avenue in Chicago. This location is now home to Mission of Our Lady of the Angels, 3808 West Iowa Street. A memorial is located on site. www.missionola.com. Queen of Heaven Cemetery is located at 1400 S Wolf Rd in Hillside, Illinois.

CHICAGO – LINCOLN PARK

Biograph Theater

The Biograph is renowned for an event that actually took place outside the theater; it is where John Dillinger, famed bank robber, was gunned down by the FBI. On July 22, 1934, Dillinger went to see *Manhattan Melodrama* with his girlfriend Polly and her landlady Anna. Anna had made a deal with the FBI to give up Dillinger that night, and she wore a bright, orange-red dress so he could be identified by the men waiting outside. Shot several times, Dillinger made it to a nearby alley before he collapsed and died. In the years following his death, eyewitnesses reported seeing a bluish figure reenacting the event. Today, however, many passersby report feeling cold and uneasy around that alley.

Source: Crowe, Richard T. *Chicago's Street Guide to the Supernatural*. Oak Park: Carolando Press, 2000, 2001; Kachuba, John B. *Ghosthunting Illinois*. Cincinnati: Clerisy Press, 2005.

The Biograph Theater is located at 2433 North Lincoln Avenue in Chicago and is open during regular business hours. www.victorygardens.org

Tonic Room

Ever since the Roaring '20s, the building now home to the Tonic Room has had a colorful history that lends itself to tales of the paranormal. A brothel was once located in the upstairs apartments, and the tavern was a popular hangout for a North Side Irish gang. When they first opened their establishment, the owners of the Tonic Room discovered Egyptian iconography painted on the basement ceiling and a pentagram painted on the basement floor, leading to speculation that it had been a meeting place for an American chapter of the Golden Dawn. One elderly woman claimed to have witnessed a ritual murder there in the 1930s when she accompanied her father to a secret meeting. According to author Ursula Bielski, patrons and staff have reported seeing apparitions in both the basement and the main bar.

Source: Bielski, Ursula. *Chicago Haunts 3: Locked Up Stories from an October City*. Holt: Thunder Bay Press, 2009.

The Tonic Room is located at 2447 North Halsted Street in Chicago and is open during regular business hours. www.thetonicroom.com

CHICAGO – LITTLE ITALY

Holy Family Church

Built between 1857 and 1859, Holy Family Church was one of the only buildings of its kind to survive the Chicago fire. Its very origins were connected to the spiritual. According to Father McCarthy, the church's pastor in 1973, its altar was positioned above a stream that ran under the church, which itself was considered sacred ground by Americans Indians because of a battle that took place there. Traditionally, divine intervention is credited for preventing the church from being consumed in the Chicago fire, since Holy Family is located only a few blocks from where popular belief asserts the fire started. Additionally, statues of two boys holding candles hang high above the altar. These are thought to be representations of the spirits of two altar boys that led a priest to a dying woman in need of receiving last rites. Once, Father McCarthy also witnessed a figure standing in the choir loft, although it had been closed to the public for years.

Source: Crowe, Richard T. *Chicago's Street Guide to the Supernatural*. Oak Park: Carolando Press, 2000, 2001; Markus, Scott. *Voices from the Chicago Grave: They're Calling. Will You Answer?* Holt: Thunder Bay Press, 2008.

Holy Family Church is located at 1080 West Roosevelt Road in Chicago. www.holyfamilychicago.org

CHICAGO – LOOP

Congress Plaza Hotel

The Congress Plaza Hotel has the nefarious distinction of being one of Chicago's largest and most haunted hotels. According to Ursula Bielski, some even believe one of its rooms inspired Stephen King's short story "1408." Since 1893, the Congress has played host to gangsters, celebrities, millionaires, and presidents. In recent years, it has suffered from the longest hotel employee strike in history. Its ghosts are numerous. Security guards have heard organ music and the sound of skate wheels sliding across the floor in the Florentine Room, a former roller skating rink, after the guests have gone to bed. Wedding attendees have gone missing from photographs taken around the grand piano in the Gold Room, and a one-legged man has been seen in the south tower. In the north tower, moans have been heard coming from the elevator on the fifth floor. Finally, the twelfth floor is believed to be home to a room so frightening that its door has been permanently sealed and hidden behind wallpaper.

Source: http://www.shermanstravel.com/top_tens/Haunted_Hotels/; Bielski, Ursula. *Chicago Haunts 3: Locked Up Stories from an October City*. Holt: Thunder Bay Press, 2009.

The Congress Plaza Hotel is located at 520 S Michigan Ave in Chicago and is open during regular business hours. www.congressplazahotel.com

Ford/Oriental Theater

This theater has had many names—Iroquois, Oriental, Ford—but none have been able to erase the stain of tragedy from this place. On December 30, 1903, five weeks after the Iroquois' grand opening, the worst theater fire in American history tore through the building, claiming the lives of 572 people. Another 30 later died of their injuries. In the alley behind the theater, 125 bodies were piled up, some of them after having leapt to their deaths from the fire escape. Today, the area is relatively quiet, but residents of the building behind the theater occasionally report feelings of uneasiness as well as unexplained sounds they believe are tied to this disaster.

Source: Bielski, Ursula. *Chicago Haunts: Ghostlore of the Windy City*. Chicago: Lake Claremont Press, 1998; Taylor, Troy. *Haunted Illinois: Travel Guide to the History and Hauntings of the Prairie State*. Alton: Whitechapel Productions Press, 2004.

The Ford Center for the Performing Arts is located at 24 W. Randolph Street near the intersection of Randolph and N. State Street, just south of the Chicago River. The theater is open during regular show times.

CHICAGO – NEAR NORTH SIDE

Old Chicago Water Tower

Constructed with limestone quarried in nearby Lemont in 1869, this unique water tower was the only structure in downtown Chicago to survive the Great Fire of 1871. Surprisingly, its resident ghost has nothing to do with the fire. In the evening, several visitors have seen lights and open windows at the top of the tower, but there are no offices up there that would explain the phenomenon. Another older ghost story associated with the tower is that the shadow of a hanged man can be seen in the windows. This was a popular tale before 1900, but there have been no recent sightings.

Source: Crowe, Richard T. *Chicago's Street Guide to the Supernatural*. Oak Park: Carolando Press, 2000, 2001.

The Old Chicago Water Tower is located in Water Tower Square along N. Michigan Avenue between E. Pearson Street and E. Chicago Avenue.

Chicago – North Center

Saint Benedict Church

St. Benedict Church was built in 1918 to serve the area's German-American residents. Stained-glass windows and ornate Stations of the Cross were even imported from Germany. According to Chicago-area ghost and folklore expert Ursula Bielski, the church's haunted history can be traced back to its construction when a worker fell from the scaffolding to his death near the altar. Since that time, an apparition of the worker has been seen sitting in the front pews or standing behind the columns in back of the altar. A janitor has also heard the sound of a kneeler rising and falling as he unlocked the church for early morning mass.

Source: Bielski, Ursula. *Chicago Haunts 3: Locked Up Stories from an October City*. Holt: Thunder Bay Press, 2009.

St. Benedict Church is located at 2215 West Irving Park Road in Chicago. www.stbenedict.com

Chicago – North Park

Bohemian Cemetery

Bohemian Cemetery is one of Chicagoland's most beautiful graveyards, with hundreds of life-sized and life-like sculptures. Started in 1877 with the burial of an infant girl, this cemetery—as its name implies—primarily served the Czech residents of Chicago. "Walking Death" is perhaps its most famous monument. Designed by Albin Polasek, it is a bronze statue, now stained green, of an elderly woman walking toward the mausoleum belonging to the Stejskal-Buchal family. Her face is covered in a hood and she walks with a staff. This cemetery also contains Civil War and Spanish-American War memorials.

Source: Hucke, Matt and Ursula Bielski. *Graveyards of Chicago: The People, History, Art, and Lore of Cook County Cemeteries.* Chicago: Lake Claremont Press, 1999; Markus, Scott. *Voices from the Chicago Grave: They're Calling. Will You Answer?* Holt: Thunder Bay Press, 2008.

Bohemian National Cemetery is located at 5255 N. Pulaski Road just west of Northeastern Illinois University. The cemetery closes at dusk.

LaBaugh Woods

LaBuagh Woods sits across the railroad tracks west of a group of large graveyards that includes Bohemian Cemetery. It is a claustrophobic forest and park that is divided by the Des Plaines River. Known for its gang activity, it also has a sinister reputation of a different kind. Since at least the 1960s, rumors of Satanic and occult worship at LaBuagh Woods have circulated in local high schools. Today, many of the trees along its trail are tagged with graffiti.

Source: Bielski, Ursula. *Chicago Haunts: Ghostlore of the Windy City*. Chicago: Lake Claremont Press, 1998.

The entrance to LaBaugh Woods is located off N. Cicero Avenue between the I-94 exit ramp and W. Foster Avenue. The forest preserve closes at dusk.

Chicago – Norwood Park

John Wayne Gacy Home (Former)

John Wayne Gacy is a notorious name among Chicagoans. Between 1972 and 1978, Gacy raped and murdered at least 33 teenage boys and young men. He hid most of the bodies in the crawl space under his home, and the rest he buried around his property or dumped into the Des Plaines River. His crimes, which shocked the nation, were made all the more horrible because of Gacy's charity performances as "Pogo the Clown," which won him the nickname the "killer clown." He was convicted of 33 murders on March 13, 1980, and executed by lethal injection on May 10, 1994. Meanwhile, a strange phenomenon was reported at his former home. The house had been demolished in 1979, but the area where the bodies were discovered remained barren years after they were exhumed. The quicklime Gacy spread to mask the smell of decay was ruled out as a culprit, since police had extensively churned up the soil in their search for evidence. It was as though the vegetation itself was repelled by the horror of what happened. Eventually, the lot was sold and a new home built at the location. Since that time, everything appears to have returned to normal.

Source: Bielski, Ursula. *Chicago Haunts 3: Locked Up Stories from an October City*. Holt: Thunder Bay Press, 2009; Crowe, Richard T. *Chicago's Street Guide to the Supernatural*. Oak Park: Carolando Press, 2000, 2001.

The John Wayne Gacy Home was formerly located at 8213 W. Summerdale Avenue in Chicago, near the intersection of Summerdale and Courtland Ave. This is a private residential neighborhood.

CHICAGO - RIVER NORTH

Excalibur Club

Constructed from rough granite blocks that give it a castle-like appearance, this Romanesque Revival building has had a long and colorful history. Built in 1892 by the Chicago Historical Society, since 1931 it has been home to the Loyal Order of the Moose, the WPA, a technology institute, a magazine company, and finally, a nightclub called the Limelight. When the Limelight opened, its staff almost immediately noticed unusual activity, especially on the third floor. On the pool table, balls rolled around on their own. The sound of heavy boxes moving in the storage room was often heard, even though the room was locked and empty.

Hauntings continued when the club became the Excalibur in 1990. One bartender was reportedly trapped in a bathroom stall for several minutes, as though someone was holding the door closed. On one visit, Scott Markus claimed to hear keys rattling and witnessed a figure that seemed to vanish behind a support column. Thanks to these and many similar incidents, the Excalibur is a favorite subject around Halloween for local radio and news stations.

Source: Crowe, Richard T. *Chicago's Street Guide to the Supernatural*. Oak Park: Carolando Press, 2000, 2001; Markus, Scott. *Voices from the Chicago Grave: They're Calling. Will You Answer?* Holt: Thunder Bay Press, 2008.

The Excalibur Club is located at 632 North Dearborn Street in Chicago and is open during regular business hours. www.excaliburchicago.com.

CHICAGO - STREETERVILLE

Drake Hotel

The opening night of the Drake Hotel was both magnificent and tragic. It was magnificent because the Drake was to be one of Chicago's most beautiful hotels; it was tragic because, according to legend, it was the night the "Woman in Red" ended her life. On New Year's Eve in 1920, a man and his fiancée (who was clad in a brilliant silk gown) attended the gala held in the Drake's Gold Coast Room on opening night. The man stepped away and did not return, so his fiancée went looking for him. She found him, enthralled by another woman, in the Palm Court parlor. Devastated, the Woman in Red climbed to the roof and jumped to her death. Since then, guests at the Drake have reported seeing her ghost in the Gold Coast Room, Palm Court, on the top floor, and the roof. She seems to be condemned to replay her final night.

Source: Bielski, Ursula. *Chicago Haunts 3: Locked Up Stories from an October City*. Holt: Thunder Bay Press, 2009.

The Drake Hotel is located at 140 East Walton Place in Chicago and is open during regular business hours. www.thedrakehotel.com

Chicago – Uptown

Graceland Cemetery

Graceland is one of the oldest and most famous of Chicago's graveyards. It was established in 1860 when overcrowding and unsanitary conditions in Chicago's original cemetery forced the city to move the bodies to a new location. Some of the wealthiest and most powerful Chicagoans are buried here, but two monuments in particular stand out in local lore. The first, a bronze statue of a cloaked figure called "Eternal Silence" marks the burial place of Dexter Graves. According to legend, visitors who look into the face of the cloaked figure will be granted a vision of their own death. It is also said that no pictures can be taken of the monument, but this is certainly untrue.

The second legend concerns the statue of a young girl reclining in a chair, encased in glass. The statue is a life-size recreation of Inez Clark, who was six years old when she died. Not much is known about her life, but there are many reports of her statue vanishing from inside the glass case. Stranger still, Helen Sclair, a local cemetery expert, believes that Inez Clark is not buried at that location and that the statue was a gift to the Clarks from the sculptor, A. Gagel. Whether or not Inez's mortal remains are at rest under her statue, it continues to be a place of pilgrimage for many Chicagoans.

Source: Crowe, Richard T. *Chicago's Street Guide to the Supernatural*. Oak Park: Carolando Press, 2000, 2001; Hucke, Matt and Ursula Bielski. *Graveyards of Chicago: The People, History, Art, and Lore of Cook County Cemeteries*. Chicago: Lake Claremont Press, 1999.

Graceland Cemetery is located at 4001 N. Clark Street, between W. Montrose Avenue and W. Irving Park Road. The cemetery closes at dusk.

CHICAGO – WEST ELSDON

Lourdes High School (Former)

Richard T. Crowe, Chicago's most respected authority on local ghost lore, taught English and journalism at Lourdes High School in 1972/73. During that time, he heard stories about a nun who haunted the third floor. Tales of the phantom nun had been told for decades. Heavy footsteps were sometimes heard echoing down the empty corridor, and a ghostly specter was seen on more than one occasion. Stitch Hall, an auditorium added during the 1950s, also reportedly experienced this activity. Several years ago, Lourdes closed and John Hancock High School opened in its place. It is unknown whether the ghostly activity has continued.

Source: Crowe, Richard T. *Chicago's Street Guide to the Supernatural*. Oak Park: Carolando Press, 2000, 2001.

Lourdes High School is now John Hancock High School, which is located at 4034 W. 56th Street in Chicago. The school is not open to the public.
www.hancockhs.org

Evanston

Calvary Cemetery

This picturesque resting ground along the shore of Lake Michigan is home to the tale of "the Aviator," or as he is sometimes affectionately known, "Seaweed Charlie." Between the late 1950s and 1960s, some passersby were treated to the alarming sight of a man drowning far out of reach in the icy waters. Even more startling was what came next. Instead of disappearing under the waves to a watery grave, the man, usually disheveled but sometimes covered in seaweed, emerged from the lake and crawled over the rocks toward the gate of Calvary Cemetery before ultimately vanishing. This scene was replayed many times before finally, one night after cemetery caretakers accidentally left the gate open, the ghost disappeared forever. Despite this apparent end, sporadic sightings continued into the late '90s.

Source: Bielski, Ursula. *Chicago Haunts: Ghostlore of the Windy City.* Chicago: Lake Claremont Press, 1998; Crowe, Richard T. *Chicago's Street Guide to the Supernatural.* Oak Park: Carolando Press, 2000, 2001; Kleen, Michael. "Calvary Cemetery." *Legends and Lore of Illinois* 2 (June 2008): 1-7.

Calvary Cemetery is located at 301 Chicago Avenue, just west of Sheridan Road and Lake Michigan. There is an entrance off both Chicago and Sheridan streets. The cemetery closes at dusk.

68 | *Michael Kleen*

HOFFMAN ESTATES

Shoe Factory Road

The most distinctive feature on Shoe Factory Road in Hoffman Estates used to be an old, derelict Spanish Colonial revival style building. Just down the street, in the direction of the Poplar Creek Forest preserve, sat an abandoned farm. Both were rumored to be haunted. The unique, stone house was at one time the Charles A. Lindbergh School, named after the famed aviator. According to local historian John Russell Ghrist, the current structure was built in 1929. The school closed in 1948 when rural schools began to be consolidated into the modern Illinois public school system. It spent the next 30 years as a residence until it became abandoned sometime during the late 1980s.

Some local teens believed that the stone house became abandoned after a child living in the home killed his parents. They claim the ghost of this child, who plays with a knife, could be seen sitting on the steps. The haunted farm, and its nefarious barn, had several stories associated with it. One story involved the farmer going insane and murdering his family, then burying them in the middle of a circle of trees. The other had the family being murdered and hung in the barn by a mental patient. Both of these buildings were torn down in 2007.

Source: Brooks, Rachel. *Chicago Ghosts*. Atglen: Schiffer Books, 2008; Kleen, Michael. *Paranormal Illinois*. Atglen: Schiffer Publishing, 2010.

The old Lindbergh School and the abandoned farm used to be located along Shoe Factory Road, just west of Rohrssen Road. They have been plowed over to make room for yet another subdivision.

Haunting Illinois: Chicagoland | 69

JUSTICE

Archer Cemetery

Archer Woods Cemetery sits near to Archer Avenue and was used for many years as the county's potter's field, where anonymous and unclaimed remains were laid to rest. An old story handed down from past generations is that this cemetery is home to the ghost of a woman in white. Like the sobbing woman of Bachelor's Grove, it is likely that this spirit is in search of a lost child or lover. On the west side of the cemetery there is a strange looking monument called the "Garden of Hymns." It is a block of sandstone slabs with several metal pipes jutting out from it, which were fashioned to look like part of a pipe organ. Rumors say organ music can be heard coming from the area on clear nights.

Source: Kleen, Michael. *Paranormal Illinois*. Atglen: Schiffer Publishing, 2010; Markus, Scott. *Voices from the Chicago Grave: They're Calling. Will You Answer?* Holt: Thunder Bay Press, 2008.

Archer Woods Cemetery is located along Kean Avenue just east of Buffalo Woods Forest Preserve. The cemetery closes at dusk.

Resurrection Cemetery

Every year, thousands of motorists drive past the gates of Resurrection Cemetery, hoping to catch a glimpse of a girl named Mary and offer her a ride. Resurrection Mary, as she is known, is hands-down the most famous legend in the Chicagoland area. She is the subject of a novel, songs, two films, and an indispensable part of any book on Chicago hauntings. Folklorists and ghost enthusiasts alike claim that Mary's story dates back to

70 | *Michael Kleen*

the 1930s, when the ghost of a burgeoning Polish girl was first seen along Archer Avenue near Resurrection Cemetery.

Mary, if she does exist, is one of the only ghosts to have ever left physical evidence behind. In 1976, a Justice police officer responded to a trespassing call and discovered two of the bars on the cemetery gate burnt and bent irregularly, with what looked like finger impressions melted into the bronze. As crowds began to gather, the Cemetery Board tried to smooth the bars with blowtorches, which only made them more conspicuous. Finally, they removed the bars altogether and sent them off to be straightened. The bars were put back in December 1978, but the discoloration remained. The cemetery has since replaced the entire gate.

Source: Bielski, Ursula. *Chicago Haunts: Ghostlore of the Windy City.* Chicago: Lake Claremont Press, 1998; Crowe, Richard T. *Chicago's Street Guide to the Supernatural.* Oak Park: Carolando Press, 2000, 2001; Kleen, Michael. *Paranormal Illinois.* Atglen: Schiffer Publishing, 2010.

Resurrection Cemetery is located along Archer Avenue (Route 171), between S. Roberts Road and Bethania Cemetery. Resurrection Mary is usually spotted along that stretch of Archer Avenue, all the way down to the Willowbrook Ballroom at 8900 Archer Avenue in Willow Springs. The cemetery closes at dusk.

Lemont

St. James-Sag

St. James of the Sag Church and Cemetery, abbreviated as St. James-Sag, sits on a bluff overlooking the juncture of the Chicago Sanitary and Ship Canal and the Calumet Sag Channel. The church and cemetery have distant origins. One burial can be traced to 1818, but the graveyard began to be heavily used in the 1830s when Father St. Cyr built a log chapel to accommodate the spiritual needs of the Irish canal workers. The limestone building that exists today was built in 1850, and in the past few decades phantom monks have made appearances here. According to Richard Crowe, a police officer by the name of Herb Roberts encountered nine of these monks in the early morning hours the day after Thanksgiving, November 1977. The officer reported that the robed figures ignored him when he ordered them to stop, and they seemed to disappear as he pursued them beyond the gates of the cemetery. No monks have ever been stationed at this parish.

Source: Bielski, Ursula. *Chicago Haunts: Ghostlore of the Windy City*. Chicago: Lake Claremont Press, 1998; Crowe, Richard T. *Chicago's Street Guide to the Supernatural*. Oak Park: Carolando Press, 2000, 2001; Kleen, Michael. *Paranormal Illinois*. Atglen: Schiffer Publishing, 2010; Kaczmarek, Dale. *Windy City Ghosts: An Essential Guide to the Haunted History of Chicago*. Oak Lawn: Ghost Research Society Press, 2005.

St. James of the Sag Church and Cemetery is located off of Archer Avenue (Route 171) just north of the convergence of Archer Avenue and 107th Street. The cemetery closes at dusk.

MIDLOTHIAN

Bachelor's Grove Cemetery

Bachelor's Grove has been a south side enigma for over three decades and is one of the most famous haunted cemeteries in America. Some say it was named after a group of single men who settled in the area around the 1830s, but a family named Batchelder owned the land. One of the most controversial sightings around Bachelor's Grove involves a phantom house. In the 1970s, Richard T. Crowe collected stories from dozens of eyewitnesses who claimed to have seen a white farmhouse at various places in the woods alongside the trail, complete with a glowing light in the window. There are several foundations and old brick wells tucked away in the woods—evidence that there were homes nearby sometime in the past.

Another popular ghost is the White Lady, or Madonna, of Bachelor's Grove, who is said to be searching for her lost infant. This ghost, or one very much like it, was supposedly captured on a now famous photograph taken using infrared film. The pond adjacent to the cemetery has its own share of legends. Stories say it was one of the hundreds of places scattered around Illinois where mobsters dumped their victims during the Roaring '20s. A policeman reportedly saw the apparition of a horse, followed by a man and a plow, walk out of the pond and cross 143rd Street. The ghost is said to belong to a farmer who drowned in the pond when his horse decided to take a swim one day, pulling him under the murky water in the process.

Source: Bielski, Ursula. *Chicago Haunts: Ghostlore of the Windy City.* Chicago: Lake Claremont Press, 1998; Crowe, Richard T. *Chicago's Street Guide to the Supernatural.* Oak Park: Carolando Press, 2000, 2001; Kleen, Michael. "Bachelor's Grove." *Legends and Lore of Illinois 1* (January 2007): 1-6.

Bachelor's Grove Cemetery is located off of 143rd Street, just east of Ridgeland Avenue. Parking is available across the street in the forest preserve lot. The cemetery closes at dusk.

NORRIDGE

Robinson Woods

Alexander Robinson (also known as Chee-Chee-Pin-Quay) was the chief of the Potawatomi, Chippewa, and Ottawa at the time of the Fort Dearborn Massacre. This land, which is now a forest preserve, was given to his family in gratitude for saving American lives during the massacre. In addition to Alexander and his French wife Catherine Chevalier, several of the Robinson kin are interred here, and a large granite memorial marks the entrance to the burial ground. When the City of Chicago annexed the land during the construction of O'Hare Airport, it promised Robinson's sole living descendent that he could be buried there with the rest of his family. When he died, however, the city broke its promise. Some local folklorists

Haunting Illinois: Chicagoland | 73

believe this might have been the beginning of the haunting. Ever since the 1960s, visitors have reported hearing sounds like drums and chopping coming from deep in the woods. The scent of freshly cut flowers has also been smelled, even in the dead of winter.

Source: Crowe, Richard T. *Chicago's Street Guide to the Supernatural*. Oak Park: Carolando Press, 2000, 2001; Kaczmarek, Dale. *Windy City Ghosts: An Essential Guide to the Haunted History of Chicago*. Oak Lawn: Ghost Research Society Press, 2005.

> Robinson Woods is located along the Des Plaines River, west of East River Road and north of W. Lawrence Avenue. The Robinson Family burial ground is located just north of that intersection. The forest preserve closes at dusk.

PALATINE

Fremd High School

Opened in 1961 to accommodate the Baby Boomers, William Fremd High School is reportedly haunted by three ghosts, one of which has roamed its halls since the 1970s. In Kolze Auditorium, seats spring up and spotlights have been known to light on their own. Another nameless phantom is said to sigh and moan in Room 122. The most infamous ghost at Fremd haunts the swimming pool, where a freshman girl died of a heart attack while swimming laps. Students claim the spot where she drowned is always much colder than the rest of the pool. Others have seen a colorful haze hovering over the water. Today, Fremd has the largest student body in the district and is recognized as one of the best high schools in the state of Illinois.

Source: Bielski, Ursula. *More Chicago Haunts: Scenes from Myth and Memory*. Chicago: Lake Claremont Press, 2000; Kaczmarek, Dale. *Windy City Ghosts II: More tales from America's most haunted city*. Oak Lawn: Ghost Research Society Press, 2005.

> William Fremd High School is located at 1000 S. Quentin Road, just south of Illinois Avenue. The building is not open to the general public.

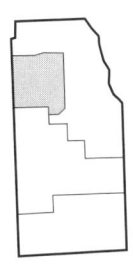

DuPage County

Population: 904,161
County Seat: Wheaton
Total Area: 337 square miles
Per capita income: $36,532
Year Established: 1839

Clarendon Hills

Country House Restaurant

It is not often that a ghost story can be tied to a real event, but the ghost who haunts the Country House in Clarendon Hills has been identified by both psychics and a former owner of the restaurant, who was there the day she died. The year was 1958. A young mother approached the restaurant's bartender and asked if he could watch her child while she ran an errand. Sensing something unusual about the request, he declined. The young woman left, never to return—at least not in life. Moments later, she committed suicide by driving into a tree. Fortunately, her child was unharmed.

Years after the incident, two brothers bought the restaurant and began to experience strange phenomenon. Guests heard their names being called, the jukebox played on its own, and employees frequently heard a woman sobbing. The new owners called in a psychic, who related the story of the woman's suicide (although she said it happened in 1957), which the original owner later confirmed.

Source: Bielski, Ursula. *Chicago Haunts: Ghostlore of the Windy City.* Chicago: Lake Claremont Press, 1998; Christensen, Jo-Anne. *Ghost Stories of Illinois.* Edmonton: Lone Pine, 2000.

The Country House is located at 241 55th Street, just east of Clarendon Hills Road. It is open during regular business hours.

Haunting Illinois: Chicagoland

ELMHURST

Wilder Mansion

Between 1922 and the autumn of 2003, the Elmhurst Public Library occupied a beautiful old building on the 200 block of Prospect Avenue known as "White Birch" or "Lancaster Lodge." This was the Wilder Mansion, named after Thomas E. Wilder, its owner at the time the Park District purchased the building for public use. Built in 1868 by Seth Wadhams, it served as a residence for over 50 years until the City of Elmhurst converted the first floor into a library. As is sometimes the case, the remodeling done to this 141 year old home has disturbed the spirit of its original owner, or so some librarians believed. Among other things, they described lights that mysteriously turned on overnight, feelings of being followed, and books that fell off shelves without perceivable cause. After the library moved to its new location, the Park District partially restored the Wilder Mansion and operates it as a rental facility for weddings and other functions.

Source: www.elmhurstpubliclibrary.org; www.wildermansion.org; Kaczmarek, Dale. *Windy City Ghosts II: More tales from America's most haunted city.* Oak Lawn: Ghost Research Society Press, 2005.

The Wilder Mansion is located at 211 Prospect Avenue, just southeast of Elmhurst College at the intersection of Prospect and Elm Park Avenue. The mansion is not open to the general public.

GLEN ELLYN

The Cursed Stone

Some people believe tokens will bring them good luck. In the 1970s, Gilbert and Trudy Woods discovered a stone behind their suburban home on Hill Avenue that had the opposite effect. Strange symbols, including what looked like a serpent, adorned its face, and the couple saw fit to add the mysterious object to their rock garden. Poltergeist activity soon followed, along with a series of unexpected medical crises. After Gilbert had a heart attack and Trudy developed Multiple Sclerosis, they decided to give the stone to a friend, who also began to have bad luck. As their story spread, the stone attracted the attention of the local news and the New Age community. The stone passed from one owner to another, always leaving a trail of unfortunate events in its wake.

Source: Kaczmarek, Dale. *Windy City Ghosts: An Essential Guide to the Haunted History of Chicago*. Oak Lawn: Ghost Research Society Press, 2005.

LISLE

Benedictine University

Benedictine University is a private, Catholic university with a student population of around 5,000. Its current campus was built in 1901 at the beginning of the Edwardian era, after having been located on the Lower West Side of Chicago since 1887. Originally known as St. Procopius College, it changed its name to Illinois Benedictine College in 1971 and then to Benedictine University in 1996. Students at the college believe its imposing halls, woods, and cemetery are haunted by tortured ghosts. They speak of rituals in the woods where a woman's body was once discovered, and of the death of a student who committed suicide by lying in the street. Lake Saint Benedict, a swampy, kidney-shaped slough next to the cemetery, only adds to this atmosphere.

According to both Ursula Bielski and Dale Kaczmarek, several students have attempted to contact the ghost of a former monk via Ouija Board, with disastrous results. A young lady living in Neuzil Residence Hall, for instance, blamed a séance gone wrong for a fire that started in her room, and several boys were scared witless after they brought a Ouija Board to the cemetery. These events took place during the early 1990s as the school entered its second century in operation.

Haunting Illinois: Chicagoland

Source: Bielski, Ursula. *Chicago Haunts: Ghostlore of the Windy City*. Chicago: Lake Claremont Press, 1998; Kaczmarek, Dale. *Windy City Ghosts: An Essential Guide to the Haunted History of Chicago*. Oak Lawn: Ghost Research Society Press, 2005.

Benedictine University is located at 5700 College Road southwest of College and Maple Avenue in Lisle.

NAPERVILLE

1946 Naperville Train Disaster

On the afternoon of April 26, 1946, the engineer of a Chicago, Burlington, and Quincy Railroad passenger train, the Advance Flyer, made an unscheduled stop at the Naperville station to check his running gear. This proved to be a fatal mistake because another passenger train, the Exposition Flyer, came barreling toward him at 85mph. By the time the engineer of the Exposition Flyer realized what was happening, it was too late. The resulting collision destroyed both trains, killed 47 passengers, and injured around 125 others. The nearby Kroehler building, a furniture manufacturer, became a make-shift morgue and its employees became rescue volunteers. Because of this accident, passenger trains in the United States now only travel at or below 79mph. According to Kevin Frantz, proprietor of Ghost Tours of Naperville, eyewitnesses have seen lost and disoriented specters walking along Loomis Street. Residents of 4th Avenue, where bodies were laid out right after the crash, have also allegedly experienced cold spots, strange noises, and shadows.

Source: Frantz, Kevin J. Naperville, *Chicago's Haunted Heighbor, Vol. 1*. Naperville: Unrested Dead Publishing, 2008; Ladley, Diane A. *Haunted Naperville*. Chicago: Acadia Publishing, 2009; http://www3.gendisasters.com/illinois/7341/naperville-il-disastrous-train-wreck-apr-1946.

The wreck occurred at the intersection of the railroad tracks and Loomis Street, just east of the Amtrak/Metra station in Naperville.

Barbara Pfeiffer Hall and Theater

Founded in 1861 as Plainfield College and originally located in Plainfield, North Central College was moved to Naperville in 1870. In 1926, a new arts building was added to the campus and named after Barbara Pfeiffer, the mother of a prominent benefactor. Over the next eight decades, the Pfeiffer Theater developed quite a reputation for playing host to as many as a half dozen ghosts. The most well-known of these is that of an elderly lady dressed in an elegant white dress who is said to have died in seat G-42. Mysterious faces have appeared in photographs taken in the balcony and lighting booth, and students report feelings of being watched in that booth. Other ghosts include a drama teacher who is believed to have committed suicide and a former janitor named "Charlie." He haunts the west stairwell and balcony.

Source: Ladley, Diane A. *Haunted Naperville*. Chicago: Acadia Publishing, 2009; Norman, Michael. *Haunted Homeland: A Definitive Collection of North American Ghost Stories*. New York: Tor Books, 2006.

North Central College is located at 30 North Brainard Street, off Chicago Avenue. Barbara Pfeiffer Memorial Hall is located at the corner of Brainard and Van Buren.
www.northcentralcollege.edu

WAYNE

Munger Road

Like Barrington's Cuba Road, Munger Road sits at the periphery of the Chicago Suburbs and has attracted a number of strange legends. The road itself penetrates deep into Pratts Wayne Woods. Motorists have reported being chased by a wolf with glowing red eyes as well as a vanishing Oldsmobile. Perhaps the most famous legend centers on the now-defunct railroad track that intersects with Munger.

Haunting Illinois: Chicagoland | 79

The legend is a familiar one: three children pushed a baby carriage across the tracks just in time to save it from a passing train. Unfortunately, the children were killed. Today, if your car happens to stall on the tracks, phantom hands will push it to safety. While that is a common rural legend, a train did derail nearby. According to a former forest preserve employee interviewed by Ursula Bielski, an old abandoned house also sat north of the railroad tracks. Its owners left after a fire, and vandals and curious teens moved in. Naturally, they claimed the house was inhabited by Satan worshippers. The house was demolished in 2000.

Source: Bielski, Ursula. *Chicago Haunts 3: Locked Up Stories from an October City*. Holt: Thunder Bay Press, 2009.

Munger Road runs north and south between W. Steams Rd. and Smith Road, east of St. Charles and west of Route 59.

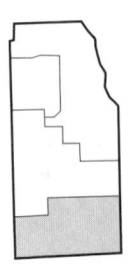

KANKAKEE COUNTY

Population: 103,833
County Seat: Kankakee
Total Area: 681 square miles
Per capita income: $19,055
Year Established: 1834

MANTENO

Manteno State Hospital

Manteno State Hospital opened its doors in the early 1930s as construction on the sprawling hospital was still ongoing. Like Peoria (Bartonville) State Hospital, Manteno was laid out in a "cottage plan," which meant that the patients were housed in a series of separate buildings rather than in one single institution. When it first opened, Manteno accommodated 6,620 total residents. Underground service tunnels linked all the buildings. In 1939, in an incident that *Time* magazine referred to as the "Manteno Madness," 384 patients and staff came down with typhoid fever and more than 50 ultimately died.

Manteno State Hospital was later renamed the Manteno Mental Health Center and closed in 1985. The north side of campus became a veteran's home. Other buildings were consolidated into the Illinois Diversatech Campus and rented to businesses. The main administration building became a bank. Despite public health concerns, a housing project called Fairway Oaks Estates was recently built at the location. Since the hospital's closure, many people have visited its remains and have come away with strange stories. They have seen apparitions of patients and nurses and have heard voices over the long-defunct intercom.

Source: Kleen, Michael. *Paranormal Illinois*. Atglen: Schiffer Publishing, 2010; Taylor, Troy. *Haunted Illinois: The Travel Guide to the History & Hauntings of the Prairie State*. Alton: Whitechapel Productions Press, 2004.

Manteno State Hospital was located off N 4000E Road, just southeast of Manteno. To find the old hospital buildings, turn down Diversitech Drive. The subdivision will be on your left. Some of the cottages still remain, but they are occupied by private businesses.

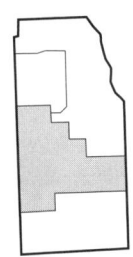

WILL COUNTY

Population: 502,266
County Seat: Joliet
Total Area: 849 square miles
Per capita income: $24,613
Year Established: 1836

CRETE

Axeman's Bridge

There's nothing unusual about the concrete bridge over Plum Creek along Old Post Road. In the woods to the northeast, however, sits a rickety steel bridge, currently collapsed into the water. It is tagged with graffiti. For years, local teens imagined that this was the scene of a gruesome axe murder. Some said the Axeman (or Ax-Man) killed a group of kids he caught trespassing on his property.

Others tied the tale to the abandoned house nearby, claiming that the man had chopped up his family and then murdered two police officers who came to investigate. When backup arrived, they chased the man to the old steel bridge, where they shot him dead. Today, there are still remains of a house scattered in the woods.

Source: Kaczmarek, Dale. *Windy City Ghosts: An Essential Guide to the Haunted History of Chicago*. Oak Lawn: Ghost Research Society Press, 2005; Kleen, Michael. "Axeman's Bridge." *Legends and Lore of Illinois* 3 (December 2009): 1-8.

Axeman's Bridge is located in the woods northeast of the concrete bridge along Old Post Road. From the Calumet Expressway, go east on Richton Road and turn right on Old Post.

Monee Road and Sangamon Street

Three phantoms have been seen on and around Monee Road and Sangamon Street, south of the small town of Crete. At the Old Monee railroad crossing, eyewitnesses have reported hearing the screams of a young girl or seeing her playing on the tracks. In 2006, one visitor from Indiana told Ursula Bielski that she had nearly hit a woman and her young boy who appeared in the road during a rainstorm. She described the woman as "wild-looking" and the boy as "half-asleep." Both had vanished by the time she got out of the car to see if they were okay.

Source: Bielski, Ursula. *Chicago Haunts 3: Locked Up Stories from an October City*. Holt: Thunder Bay Press, 2009.

Sangamon Street intersects with Old Monee Road just southwest of Crete and stops at New Monee Road (Crete-Monee Road). The railroad tracks are located just west of Sangamon St.

JOLIET

Frank Shaver Allen Home

Frank Shaver Allen (1860–1934) was a talented architect from Joliet who achieved national recognition for his work. While he did design a few residences, he is most known for designing public school buildings in the Richardsonian Romanesque style. He designed three of Joliet's schools: Joliet Central High, Sheridan Elementary, and Broadway. During the 1970s, Frank S. Allen's former home at the corner of Morgan Street and Dewey Avenue became the center of a local media frenzy over poltergeist activity that allegedly took place there. Several ghosts, including an elderly woman, a nanny, and a child, manifested themselves. The family living in the house also heard disembodied voices and saw fires that vanished without leaving behind any damage. The ghost of Frank Shaver Allen himself is also supposed to haunt the house. The activity seems to have died down in recent decades.

Source: http://www.cityofjoliet.com/halloffame/artists/fsallen.htm; http://theshadowlands.net/places/illinois.htm.

The Frank Shaver Allen home is located at 608 Morgan Street, just north and west of Route 52. This is a private residence.

Joliet Catholic High School (Former)

In 1990, St. Francis Academy, an all-girls school, and Joliet Catholic High, an all-boys school, merged to create Joliet Catholic Academy. Both the Carmelite Order and the Joliet Franciscan Sisters now sponsor this coed school, which is located along Larkin Avenue. The Joliet Catholic High School

Haunting Illinois: Chicagoland

building is currently a retirement home known as Victory Centre of Joliet, and its classrooms have been converted into apartments. Between 1972 and 1990 (when the school relocated), it was widely believed to be haunted by the ghost of a priest and educator named Kellen Ryan, who died in an auto accident when he fell asleep behind the wheel. Janitors claimed that lights turned on in his former classroom after hours, and they occasionally witnessed the apparition of a priest wandering the halls. Rather than a frightening presence, students and faculty alike saw the ghost of Father Ryan as a protective spirit, watching over his "Hilltoppers."

Source: http://www.illinoishsglorydays.com/id496.html; Kaczmarek, Dale. *Windy City Ghosts II: More tales from America's most haunted city.* Oak Lawn: Ghost Research Society Press, 2005.

The former Joliet Catholic High School building is located at 29 N. Broadway Street, just west of the Des Plaines River. This is a private facility.

Rialto Theatre

The Rialto Theatre was once the most magnificent movie theater in Joliet. Its construction cost nearly $2 million in 1924, and its architecture is a mix of styles leading it to be called the "Jewel of Joliet." It opened on May 24, 1926, with the silent film *Mademoiselle Modiste*. By the 1970s, however, the theater had deteriorated to the point that only a restoration campaign by the Rialto Square Arts Association saved it from demolition. Today, it is home to a performing arts center and a school of the arts. Several ghosts are thought to reside there. One, a pretty actress in her early 20s, has been seen floating around the theater while bathed in soft light. Two lovers who tumbled to their deaths are seen in the balcony. Cold Spots, unexplained noises, and moving objects have also been reported.

Source: http://www.legendsofamerica.com/il-rialtotheatreghost.html.

The Rialto Square Theatre is located at 102 North Chicago St. in Joliet. The theater is open during regular show times. Tours are offered every Tuesday at 1:30pm for $5 per person. www.rialtosquare.com

84 | *Michael Kleen*

LOCKPORT

Runyon County Forest Preserve

The Runyon Preserve, otherwise known as Runyon Park, consists of 21 acres of woodland along Fiddyment Creek. It was named after the first white settler of Lockport Township, Armstead Runyon. His family arrived in 1830, and their cemetery is located in the woods near the park. For years, visitors have brought back strange tales of disembodied voices and voices speaking in an indiscernible language. At least one of these is attributed to a witch calling out to her followers from the grave.

Source: http://www.fpdwc.org/runyon.cfm; http://theshadow lands.net/places/illinois.htm.

Runyon County Forest Preserve is located between Table, Morgan, and West streets, just west of Route 171 on the north side of Lockport. The park closes at dusk.

Haunting Illinois: Chicagoland

The Tract

Western Illinois has a peculiar and unique history. Politically and economically isolated from the rest of the state, this region was named after the Illinois Military Tract of 1812, which was a section of land set aside for veterans of the War of 1812. Prior to the 1970s, there were only five Illinois highway river bridge crossings south of Peoria, leading some to call this area "Forgottonia." In 1972, a student at Western Illinois University proclaimed himself "Governor of Forgottonia" to protest the lack of funding and attention from the Illinois legislature in Springfield. He named the tiny village of Fandon as its new capital. Today, it is still one of the most underdeveloped regions in the state.

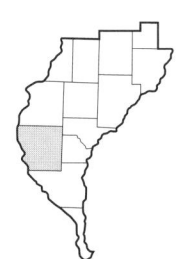

Adams County

Population: 68,277
County Seat: Quincy
Total Area: 871 square miles
Per capita income: $17,894
Year Established: 1825

Burton Township

Burton Cave

Ever since its discovery by H.L. Tandy in 1832, Burton Cave has been plagued by rumors of strange and alarming apparitions. During a picnic in the 1880s, visitors noticed a light emanating from the cave and went to investigate. They claimed that a man wearing a black robe dashed from the entrance, and when the startled picnickers peered inside, they saw a woman, dead, covered in a white robe. Candles surrounded her body. When the local sheriff arrived, however, the strange scene had vanished. After that, locals often told tales of ghosts inhabiting the cave. Burton Cave is now part of a scenic nature preserve, and its deepest area is sealed off to protect the endangered species of bats that live there.

Source: Lewis, Chad and Terry Fisk. *The Illinois Road Guide to Haunted Locations*. Eau Claire: Unexplained Research Publishing, 2007; Scott, Beth and Michael Norman. *Haunted Heartland: True Ghost Stories from the American Midwest*. New York: Barnes & Noble Books, 1985, 1992.

Burton Cave is located in the Burton Cave Nature Preserve, east of Interstate 172 and north of Route 96. Entrance to the preserve is located off County Road 1350E.

Kingston

Haunted Cabin

As the twentieth century dawned, a young couple and their infant child found their way to an abandoned cabin on the outskirts of Kingston. Having nowhere else to go, they decided to squat there for the day. When the husband left to ask their new neighbor for work, the apparition of an old man appeared before his wife. She was afraid, but the ghost told her not to worry, that he had once owned the cabin, and that thieves had murdered him and his wife and stuffed their bodies in a nearby cave. The ghost explained that the thieves had not found their money, which he had buried beneath the floor. If the young couple would only lay the bones of the old man and his wife to rest, they could have the money. Incredibly, when the woman dug where the old man's ghost indicated, she uncovered a box filled with coins and rolled greenbacks. When her husband returned, she explained what happened. The two made straightaway for the cave, where they found the bones of the elderly couple and then buried them in a nearby cemetery. The young couple stayed in the cabin, and the ghost of the old man never bothered them again.

Source: Christensen, Jo-Anne. *Ghost Stories of Illinois*. Edmonton: Lone Pine, 2000; Hyatt, Harry Middleton. *Folk-lore from Adams County, Illinois*. Alma Egan Hyatt Foundation, 1935.

Quincy

Quincy Junior High

The middle school years are generally a tough time for adolescents, and for some, the stress can be too much to bear. For students of Quincy Junior High, their angst has been personified in the ghost of a young boy who, according to legend, hung himself in one of the bathrooms after being dumped by his girlfriend. Every year on the anniversary of his death, students and teachers are said to hear footsteps, crying, and mumbling in the bathroom. Students claim that teachers have kept quiet about the boy's death in order to prevent copycats. Quincy Junior High occupies a beautiful old building that was constructed in 1933 and served as Quincy's high school between 1933 and 1957.

Source: http://theshadowlands.net/places/illinois.htm.

Quincy Junior High School is located at 100 S. 14th Street between Main and Jersey streets. The school is not open to the general public.

CALHOUN COUNTY

Population: 5,084
County Seat: Hardin
Total Area: 284 square miles
Per capita income: $16,785
Year Established: 1825

HARDIN

Diamond Island Phantom

During the 1880s, dozens of eyewitnesses saw a strange fireball on an island in the Illinois River a short distance from the town of Hardin. Two boys first witnessed the fireball in 1885 while fishing on the shore across from the island. The bright light shot out of the trees and hovered along the riverbank, sending the boys fleeing for home. Over the next few years, many reputable people witnessed the phenomenon, but others remained skeptical. The skeptics decided to camp out on the island and prove the whole thing was a hoax. After a few hours, the orange fireball appeared and flew over their heads, ultimately landing in one of their boats where—they claimed—it transformed into an old man wearing overalls before it ultimately vanished. The phantom was never seen again.

Source: Taylor, Troy. *Haunted Illinois: The Travel Guide to the History & Hauntings of the Prairie State*. Alton: Whitechapel Productions Press, 2004.

Diamond Island is located in the Illinois River north of Hardin, off of Illinois River Road.

Haunting Illinois: The Tract

Fulton County

Population: 38,250
County Seat: Lewistown
Total Area: 883 square miles
Per capita income: $17,373
Year Established: 1823

Farmington

The Farrington Brothers' Gold

Outlaws became national folk heroes after the Civil War, when irregular guerrillas and veterans of the Confederate Cavalry used the skills they learned during the war to enrich themselves and their families at the expense of railroads and banks. Levi and Hilary Farrington were no exception. They fought with Quantrill's Raiders during the war and joined an outlaw gang after. In 1870, they robbed a train in Tennessee and made off with $20,000 in gold. During the escape, the two brothers were separated, and Levi laid low at a farm near Farmington, Illinois, where he is rumored to have hidden the gold. He was captured by a deputy after a short time and lynched in Union City, Tennessee. The Farrington Brother's loot was never found.

Source: Henson, Michael Paul. *A Guide to Treasure in Illinois and Indiana*. Dona Ana: Carson Enterprises, 1982.

Farmington is located directly west of Peoria along Route 116.

Lewistown

Dickson Mounds

Located at the juncture of the Illinois and Spoon Rivers, Dickson Mounds was a settlement site of Mississippian Indians, as well as the Oneota tribe, and was named for the Dickson family, who purchased the land in 1834. During the 1920s, Don Dickson, a chiropractor and amateur archaeologist, began to excavate the site and turned it into a private museum. It quickly became popular and was added to the National Register of Historic Places in 1972. In the early 1990s, former Governor Jim Edgar ordered the Amerindian remains be re-covered and a new museum was built at the location. Recently, archeologists from the Dickson Mounds Museum discovered evidence of a 700 year old settlement near the mounds, which included pottery shards, arrowheads, and human bones.

Source: "700-year-old settlement unearthed near Dickson Mounds," *Journal Star* (Peoria) 19 June 2009; http://www.lib.niu.edu /2001/oi0111 06.html.

Dickson Mounds State Park is located at 10956 N. Dickson Mounds Road, southeast of Lewistown. The park closes at dusk.

The Phantom Steamboat

Tales of phantom ships frequently grace the coasts of Florida and the Carolinas, but such things are not unheard of in Illinois. Until the advent of automobiles and air travel, riverboats were a primary mode of travel and a common sight on Illinois waterways. Fulton County is home to a phantom riverboat that makes its appearance whenever the waters of the Spoon River swell. The legend began in the late 1840s, when an inexperienced riverboat crew attempted to navigate the river during a flood. The sound of a whistle and the passengers singing "Sweet By and By" was the last the townsfolk ever heard of the vessel, that is, until a few years later.

In 1853, during another flood, eyewitnesses heard the distinctive sound of a whistle blowing in the fog. They rushed to the river's edge and saw the same boat that had vanished years before. This time, it was wrapped in an eerie glow, and four, gleaming white passengers stood on deck singing "Sweet By and By." Several men attempted to approach the steamboat with a skiff, but as they got closer, the air became icy and the fog was too dense to see where they were going. The phantom vessel disappeared into the night.

Source: Christensen, Jo-Anne. *Ghost Stories of Illinois*. Edmonton: Lone Pine, 2000; Republican (St. Louis) 20 April 1889.

The Spoon River is located south and southwest of Lewistown in rural Fulton County.

Haunting Illinois: The Tract | 93

VERMONT

Effland Woods

According to legend, an old dirt road once passed through Effland Woods. One day, an accident befell a group of travelers on the road and they all died. In some versions of the story, this was a car accident. People stopped using the road, and it became swallowed up by the woods. Now, visitors to the woods claim to see floating balls of light zipping between the trees. Others have heard whistling and low voices and felt like they were being watched or followed by something unseen.

Source: Lewis, Chad and Terry Fisk. *The Illinois Road Guide to Haunted Locations*. Eau Claire: Unexplained Research Publishing, 2007; http://theshadowlands.net/places/illinois.htm.

Effland Woods is located directly south of the intersection of Quarter Road (350N) and McDonough Line Road (2400E), north of Vermont and west of Sugar Creek.

KNOX COUNTY

Population: 55,836
County Seat: Galesburg
Total Area: 720 square miles
Per capita income: $17,985
Year Established: 1825

ABINGDON

Abingdon Middle School (Former)

The old Abingdon Middle School at Snyder and Washington streets was formerly North Abingdon High School. During the 1970s, a tornado damaged the building and knocked down its distinctive chimney. Stories of the school's haunting go back decades. According to legend, a speech teacher at the high school brought her three-year-old child to work one day and left him outside to play

94 | Michael Kleen

on his tricycle while she ran into her classroom to get something. Unsupervised, her child accidentally fell down the cement steps and broke his neck. The teacher was so grief stricken that she hung herself in her classroom. Former students will swear to the truthfulness of this story. Ever since, the ghosts of both the woman and her child have been seen in and around the school, and a former janitor even reported these sightings to the police. Some storytellers claim that blood stains appear on the steps where the child died. According to writer Michelle Williams, these stories may have their roots in an actual event: the death of a teacher named Karen Moriaty in October 1956. Moriaty's tragic death is well-remembered in the community. Today, the school is abandoned and off limits to visitors.

Source: http://www.associatedcontent.com/article/392803/abin gdon_ illinois_a_haunted_town.html; http://theshadowlands.net/places/illin ois.htm.

The former Abingdon Middle School is located at 202 W. Snyder Street in Abingdon. It is closed to the general public — trespassers will be prosecuted.

The Friendly Café

After the Abingdon-based Unknown Paranormal Research Society (now the Prairieland Paranormal Society) conducted an investigation at the Friendly Café in 2009, its owners, Michael Case and Jane Voorhees, became convinced their restaurant was haunted. Michael had always suspected it was, but Jane was skeptical. Michael and the wait staff described nearly daily encounters with the paranormal to a local newspaper. "There was a woman standing in the kitchen, as clear as day," Michael told John Pulliam of the *Register-Mail*. "I couldn't see her face. I could see she had on a long dress with little pink flowers on it." At other times, he felt unseen hands pull him away from the stove. Strange encounters have also taken place in the apartments above the café. A funeral parlor was formerly located next to the restaurant, and there was a door that connected the two.

Source: "Serving Up Ghosts at a Local Diner," *Register-Mail* (Galesburg) 11 July 2009.

The Friendly Café is located at 106 S. Main Street in Abingdon and is open during regular business hours.

Galesburg

Knox College

Steeped in history, Knox College is a private liberal arts school that was founded by abolitionists in 1837. The college's Old Main building is the last remaining site of the Lincoln-Douglas debates of 1858. In 1874, Knox County built a brand new, red brick jail across the street from the college. A few years ago, Knox College purchased the jail and it is now home to the Center for Global Studies. The basement of the jail is reportedly haunted by a number of tortured spirits from the past. One prisoner, having been recaptured after an escape attempt, committed suicide in his cell. Today, university staff members have been overcome by negative feelings when they approach the old cells. Troy Taylor, after climbing into solitary confinement, found that his flashlight and camera stopped working, only to work again upon exiting the room. One unconfirmed story associated with the college itself was that a student hung himself from his dorm room window. Mistaking his body for a Halloween prank, students left it there for an entire evening before realizing their tragic error.

Source: Taylor, Troy. *Haunted Illinois: The Travel Guide to the History & Hauntings of the Prairie State*. Alton: Whitechapel Productions Press, 2004.

The old Knox County jail is located at 337 S. Cherry Street, just south of the intersection of S. Cherry and E. South Street. The Knox College campus is located west of the old jail.

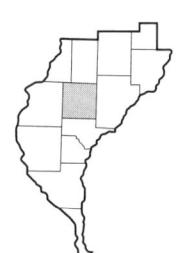

McDonough County

Population: 32,913
County Seat: Macomb
Total Area: 590 square miles
Per capita income: $15,890
Year Established: 1826

COLCHESTER

Lady in Black

Between 1898 and the first decades of the Twentieth Century, residents of the small mining town of Colchester were startled by the sudden appearance of a woman dressed in black. Her face was always covered with a black shawl. According to a local newspaper report, the first sighting took place at the corner of Hunn and Macomb streets by a woman who was walking home from church. The lady in black did not make a sound but merely followed the woman for several blocks before disappearing into thin air. The apparition was also spotted in the nearby towns of Bushnell and Macomb. According to reports in the town of Bushnell, the lady was seen "robed in deepest mourning." She appeared at all hours of the night and "in a noiseless manner." On one occasion, citizens of Bushnell even pursued the phantom, but she disappeared after a few yards. The lady in black has not been seen for at least a generation.

Source: Hallwas, John F. *McDonough County Heritage*. Macomb: Illinois Heritage Press, 1984; Moffett, Garret. *Haunted Macomb*. Charleston: The History Press, 2010; "Black Robed Ghost Haunts Illinois Town," *News* (Fort Wayne) 5 June 1902.

Colchester is located along Route 136, just west of Macomb and south of Argyle Lake State Park. Bushnell is located northeast of Macomb at the juncture of routes 9 and 41.

Haunting Illinois: The Tract | 97

Vishnu Springs

Vishnu Springs was a once-thriving resort community. Attracted to the natural spring's healing properties, an entrepreneur named Darius Hicks inherited the land and built a hotel he called the Capital Hotel. Other people soon arrived to live and work there, but the isolated nature of the resort impeded its growth. During the early 1900s, several deadly incidents and scandals tarnished the community, and when Darius Hicks committed suicide in 1908, no one remained who was willing to invest their energy in the resort. During the 1970s, a group of hippies made a short-lived attempt to turn it into a commune. Today, all that remains is the old hotel—a shadow of what it once was. Olga Kay Kennedy, a Western Illinois University alumnus, inherited Vishnu Springs from her grandparents and gifted it to the university in 2003. According to her wishes, all 140 acres will be turned into a wildlife sanctuary.

Source: "Vishnu Springs: Is the old place haunted?" *Western Courier* (Macomb) 31 October 2007; Kleen, Michael. "Vishnu Springs." *Legends and Lore of Illinois* 4 (June 2010): 1-7; Taylor, Troy. *Weird Illinois: Your Travel Guide to Illinois' Local Legends and Best Kept Secrets*. New York: Sterling Publishing, 2005.

Vishnu Springs is located at the end of a gravel drive off of E 50th Street (1100N), north of Route 136 and northwest of the Village of Tennessee. This is private property.

MACOMB

Gooseneck Ghost

The Gooseneck Ghost was the local name of a spook light that appeared along the railroad tracks just west of town in the early 1900s. It was first seen in January 1908 by a father and son who were driving a team of horses back home. The light startled their horses and they took off running.

The local newspaper described the ghost as "a bright light" and noted its proclivity for chasing travelers in that area. Looking for the Gooseneck Ghost became quite a sport for Macomb area residents, and some even brought ice cream and picnicked as they watched for it. Eventually, it was discovered that the ghost was actually a hoax that involved a Japanese lantern attached to a kite, but the prankster was never caught.

Source: "Macomb area has own ghost story," *Western Courier* (Macomb) 30 October 1991; Hallwas, John F. *McDonough County Heritage.* Macomb: Illinois Heritage Press, 1984; Moffett, Garret. *Haunted Macomb.* Charleston: The History Press, 2010.

The Gooseneck Ghost was last seen along the railroad tracks between one and two miles west of Macomb.

Illinois/Chandler Theatre (Former)

During the late 1800s, this building was a swank, small-town concert hall called the Chandler Opera House. In 1912 it was renovated and opened as the Chandler Theatre, which was renamed the Illinois Theatre in 1918. The theater showed movies in Macomb for 87 years until it finally closed in 2005. One year later, it opened as a dance club called The Forum. This building has been rumored to be haunted for several decades, and it was prominently featured in Macomb ghost tours given by Garret Moffett. During one such tour, Moffett claimed that he was attacked and pushed to the floor by unseen hands. Others have experienced uneasiness and feelings of being watched and touched without any apparent explanation.

Source: "Moffett: Paranormal Private Investigator," *Western Courier* (Macomb) 10 December 2010; Moffett, Garret. *Haunted Macomb.* Charleston: The History Press, 2010.

The Forum is located at 124 North Lafayette Street in the northwest corner of the town square in Macomb, Illinois. It is open during regular business hours.

Western Illinois University

Western Illinois University began as a teacher's college. Originally called Western Illinois State Normal School, its classes were confined to one building, now known as Sherman Hall. Sherman Hall was then known by the unimaginative title of "Main Building." In 1902 the university added a training school to Main Building in order to allow its students to obtain teaching experience in the classroom. As the student body expanded, they constructed a new building to house the training school. In the 1960s, as Western Illinois State Normal School became Western Illinois University, the Training School building was converted to house the Department of English and Journalism and renamed Simpkins Hall.

For years, students and faculty in Simpkins Hall have told stories about the ghost of an adolescent girl, but she is only one of the apparitions rumored to haunt the 71-year-old building. Many other odd occurrences at the hall are attributed to "Harold," a former janitor or graduate assistant who lurks among the classrooms on the third floor. After classes finish for the day, the disembodied sound of keys jingling, doors opening and closing, or a typewriter clicking rattle the nerves of even the most seasoned educator. Another story circulating the hall is that of a woman who can be heard crying in the first floor restroom.

Source: Kleen, Michael. *Paranormal Illinois*. Atglen: Schiffer Publishing, 2010.

*Western Illinois University is located at 1 University Circle,
on the northwest side of Macomb.*

Wigwam Hollow Cemetery

Wigwam Hollow (the colloquial name for Old Macomb Cemetery) occupies a hill on the west side of town. The first person to be interred on that hill was the daughter of Peter Hale, an early settler. She died in a fire in February 1831. As one of the oldest graveyards in the county, situated next door to Western Illinois University, Wigwam Hollow has been a Halloween tourist spot for decades. Students from the university scare themselves in night-time treks out to see the crumbling, 150 year old headstones. The hill is supposedly haunted by a man who tortured his stepdaughter to death, then escaped from jail and disappeared. Some visitors have reported hearing shrieks and groans coming from the cemetery.

Source: "Cemetery is dead, but the legend of Macomb's Wigwam Hollow lives on," *Western Courier* (Macomb) 30 October 1981; "Legend of Macomb's Wigwam Hollow lives on," *Western Courier* (Macomb) 29 October 1982.

Old Macomb Cemetery is located on a hill at the corner of Wigwam Hollow Road and W. Adams Street, at the western edge of Macomb.

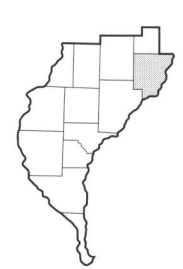

PEORIA COUNTY

Population: 182,495
County Seat: Peoria
Total Area: 631 square miles
Per capita income: $21,219
Year Established: 1825

BARTONVILLE

Peoria State Hospital

The hospital began in 1885 as Bartonville State Hospital. No patients were ever housed or treated in that building, however, and it was torn down in 1897. The institution was rebuilt and reopened in 1902 with a new name and a new superintendent. Now called Peoria State Hospital, a progressive physician named Dr. George A. Zeller took over the facility and instituted new, more humane treatments for mental illness. During his tenure there, he recorded many stories of daily life, including some that were almost beyond belief.

The main story associated with the hospital concerns the unusual circumstances surrounding the death of one of the patients, A. Bookbinder. Dr. Zeller assigned Bookbinder to the hospital's burial corps, and he performed his job admirably. Old Book, as he was sometimes called, mourned the passing of each and every person he helped inter in the cemetery. When Bookbinder died, Dr. Zeller wrote that four hundred staff and patients observed his ghost mourning at his own funeral just as he had for countless others while he was alive. They even opened the coffin to confirm that Old Book was really dead. His corpse was securely inside.

There have been other reports of paranormal experiences at Peoria State Hospital, but none of them are very specific. Recently, the Bowen Building—the main hospital building—has been opened to tours as the owners tried to raise money to restore it to its former glory.

Source: Finkler, Lauren. "Bartonville: A Broken Home Where the Haunted Roam." *Western Illinois Magazine* 1 (Spring 2010): 6-9; Lisman, Gary. *Bittersweet Memories: a History of the Peoria State Hospital*. Victoria: Trafford Publishing, 2005; Taylor, Troy. *Haunted Decatur Revisited: Ghostly Tales from the Haunted Heart of Illinois*. Alton: Whitechapel Productions Press, 2000; Zeller, George Anthony. *Befriending the Bereft*. Peoria State Hospital: by the author, 1938.

The ruins of Peoria State Hospital are located along Constitution Drive and Pfeiffer Road, just southwest of Bartonville, west of the Illinois River. The hospital sits on private property.

Peoria

The Dormitory/ Parkway Inn (Former)

In the late 1940s, Bernie Shelton, a member of the infamous Shelton gang, had aspirations to become the leading crime boss in Peoria, despite growing pressure from an alliance of St. Louis and Chicago gangsters. Carl and Bernie Shelton, brothers, both had a $10,000 price on their heads. Carl was murdered in 1947. On July 26, 1948, as Bernie was leaving the Parkway Inn (later it was called the Parkside Inn or Parkside Tavern), he was shot through the chest with a .351 Winchester Rifle by an unidentified man hiding in the woods below St. Joseph's Cemetery. He was mortally wounded and died at the hospital. By 1951, the Shelton Gang had been run out of Illinois. Since Bernie's death, however, owners and patrons of the tavern reported lights turning on and off, sudden chills, items moving, and the feeling of someone breathing on their necks. Additionally, gunshots have been heard, and patrons have reported seeing lights above the tavern coming from St. Joseph's Cemetery. The Parkside Tavern is now known as The Dormitory.

Source: McCarthy, Stephanie E. *Haunted Peoria*. Chicago: Arcadia Publishing, 2009; http://theshadowlands.net/places/illinois.htm.

The Dormitory is located at 2016 West Farmington Road, just west of Peoria across the street from Laura Bradley Park and down the hill from St. Joseph's Cemetery.

Meyer-Jacobs Theatre

Bradley University was founded in 1897 as the Bradley Polytechnic Institute. In 1908, Lydia Moss Bradley, patron of the college, paid for the construction of a beautiful gymnasium made from limestone and designed in the Gothic style. In the late 1970s, the gymnasium fell out of use and was subsequently remodeled and reopened as the Hartmann Center for the Performing Arts. A brand new theater was built inside and christened the Meyer-Jacobs Theatre. Its auditorium was impressive, with a seating capacity of 280. Something from the past, however, remained.

Since the theater opened, students have reported seeing a man in a brown suit who materializes in a cloud of cigar smoke. A second ghost, a woman wearing a white dress, has been spotted in the lobby. She appears more frequently than the brown-suited man. According to Stephanie McCarthy, the ghost of a boy who drowned in the old gymnasium pool can be heard scratching at the floor boards beneath the orchestra pit. "It's a theater building, of course we have ghosts," administrative assistant Debbie Perry recently told the *Journal Star*. In addition to its ghosts, Meyer-Jacobs Theatre is reportedly home to an impish trickster spirit that messes with the equipment. A retired theater professor called it a "whompus."

Source: McDowell, Gayle Erwin. "Hartmann Turns 100." *Bradley Hilltopics* 15 (Fall 2010): 18-19; "Peoria's Ghosts," *Journal Star* (Peoria) 31 October 2010; McCarthy, Stephanie E. *Haunted Peoria*. Chicago: Arcadia Publishing, 2009.

Meyer Jacobs Theatre is located inside the Hartmann Center for the Performing Arts at 1423 St. James Street, Bradley University.
http://slane.bradley.edu/theatre-arts/hartmann-center

Peoria Players Theatre

The Peoria Players Theatre has been in continuous operation since premiering "The Maker of Dreams" on October 6, 1919, making it the longest consecutively-running community theatre in Illinois and the fourth longest in the United States. The theater company had several homes until finally settling at their current location in 1955. The new theater had a seating capacity of 400, and its grand opening was held on November 30, 1957. Ever since Norman Endean died of cancer shortly after becoming theater manager in the 1950s, thespians at Players Theatre have encountered what many of them believed was his ghost. Lights flickered and props seemed to move on their own. Once, the grandson of a volunteer reportedly saw a man in a gray suit sitting in the auditorium. When the volunteer looked to see who it was, the auditorium was empty. A large photograph of Norm used to sit in the costume room, but it mysteriously disappeared. Several websites have incorrectly reported that Norm died onstage.

Source: "Peoria's Ghosts," *Journal Star* (Peoria) 31 October 2010; "Still Playing in Peoria," *Journal Star* (Peoria) 19 July 2008; McCarthy, Stephanie E. *Haunted Peoria*. Chicago: Arcadia Publishing, 2009; http://www.ghosttraveller.com/Illinois.htm.

The Peoria Players Theatre is located at 14300 N. University St., but it is part of the Peoria Park District's Lakeview Park and so cars must enter from W. Lake Avenue. www.peoriaplayers.org

Peoria Public Library

According to legend, the Peoria Public Library is built on cursed ground and is occupied by as many as a dozen different ghosts. Back in 1830, Mrs. Andrew Gray, a prominent Peoria citizen, lived in a house on Monroe Avenue. After her brother died, she gained custody of her nephew, who was always getting into trouble with the law. In time, he required the services of a lawyer named David Davis, who took out a mortgage on Mrs. Gray's home as security. When the bill came due, Davis sued to foreclose on the home and collect his money. Mrs. Gray was enraged. She evicted her worthless nephew, and shortly thereafter his lifeless body was found floating in the river. She then cursed the property and all its future owners. As it came to pass, misfortune befell anyone who occupied the house, including a former governor of Illinois.

In 1894, Peoria purchased the property and built a library. Contrary to some reports, the library was built next to Mrs. Gray's home, not over it. Nevertheless, the first three library directors all died under unusual circumstances. In 1966, the original library was torn down and a new one built in its place, but the ghosts remained. Employees have reportedly heard their names being called while alone in the stacks, felt cold drafts, and even claimed to have seen the face of a former library director in the basement doorway.

Source: McCarthy, Stephanie E. *Haunted Peoria*. Chicago: Arcadia Publishing, 2009; "Peoria library recipient of century old curse," *Eastern News* (Charleston) 31 October 1974.

The Peoria Public Library Main Branch is located at 107 North East Monroe Street, at the corner of Monroe and Main Street, just west of Interstate 74. The library is open during regular business hours.

Haunting Illinois: The Tract | 105

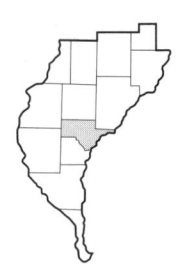

Schuyler County

Population: 7,189
County Seat: Rushville
Total Area: 441 square miles
Per capita income: $17,158
Year Established: 1825

Browning Township

Old Train Bridge

This isolated wooden bridge over the railroad tracks in rural Schuyler County is rumored to be the home of a phantom train. Locals claim that if you stand on the bridge at night, the bridge will begin to shake and you will hear a train whistle, but no train will ever arrive. Another story, common to many rural railroad bridges, is that a bus filled with children plummeted off the bridge, killing all aboard. Now the ghosts of the children can be seen darting in and out of the nearby woods. Two men in particular heard the sound of children crying while they were exploring the area.

Source: Lewis, Chad and Terry Fisk. *The Illinois Road Guide to Haunted Locations*. Eau Claire: Unexplained Research Publishing, 2007.

The old train bridge is located along Sugar Creek Bottom Road, which can be accessed via Timothy Lane off Route 24 several miles northeast of Rushville, just north of the junction of Sugar Creek and Harris Branch.

Warren County

Population: 18,735
County Seat: Monmouth
Total Area: 543 square miles
Per capita income: $16,946
Year Established: 1825

Monmouth

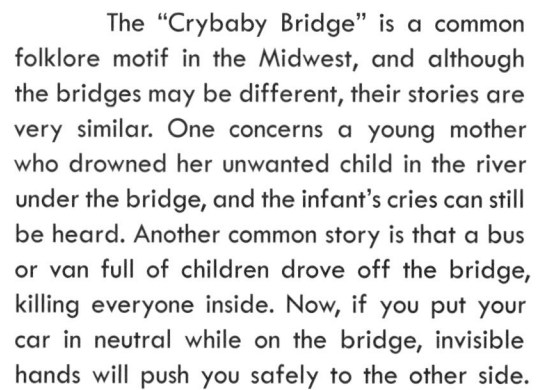

Crybaby Bridge

The "Crybaby Bridge" is a common folklore motif in the Midwest, and although the bridges may be different, their stories are very similar. One concerns a young mother who drowned her unwanted child in the river under the bridge, and the infant's cries can still be heard. Another common story is that a bus or van full of children drove off the bridge, killing everyone inside. Now, if you put your car in neutral while on the bridge, invisible hands will push you safely to the other side. Both of these legends are associated with a steel, graffiti-covered bridge in rural Warren County. One tale particular to this location involves a speeding car full of impetuous youths who struck and killed a fisherman as he cast a line into the creek. Additionally, several people have claimed to hear a baby crying near this bridge.

Source: Kleen, Michael. "Crybaby Bridge." *Legends and Lore of Illinois* 4 (July 2010): 1-7; Lewis, Chad and Terry Fisk. *The Illinois Road Guide to Haunted Locations*. Eau Claire: Unexplained Research Publishing, 2007.

Warren County's Crybaby Bridge is located north of Monmouth along 60th Street, over Cedar Creek.

Haunting Illinois: The Tract

The Heartland

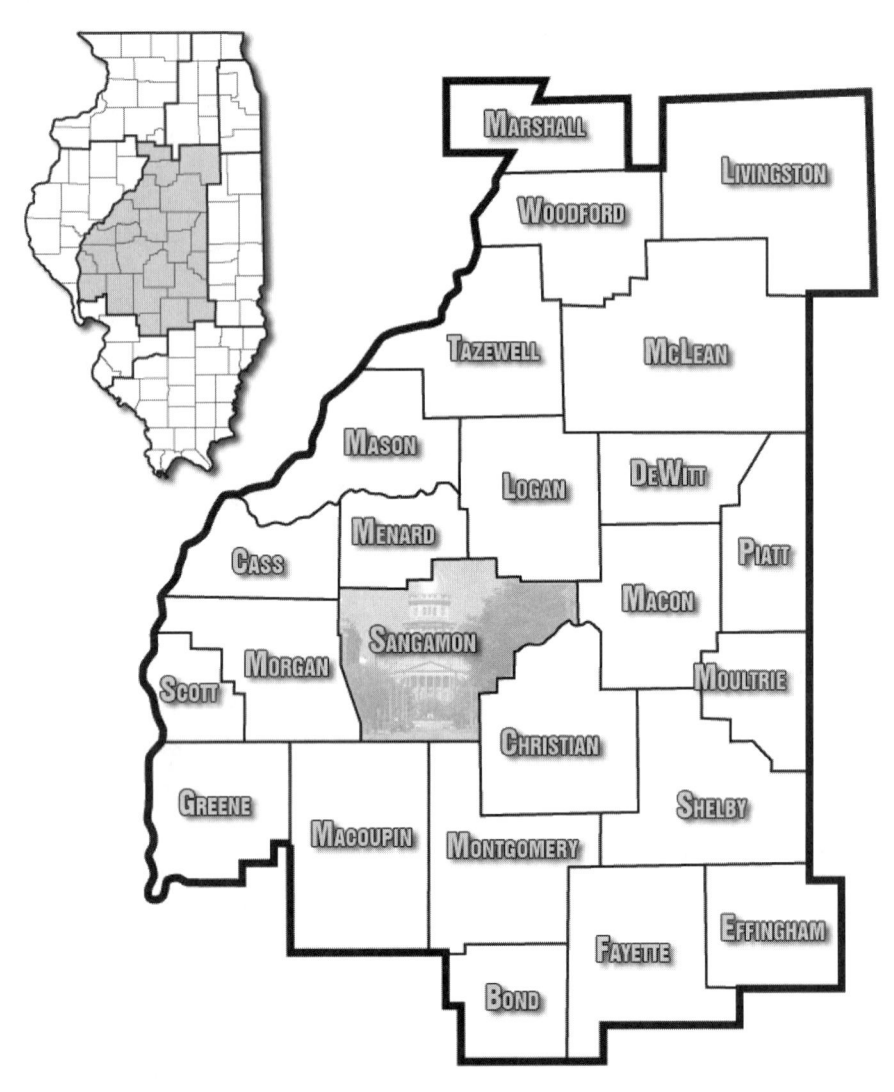

The Heartland of Illinois is distinguished by its rich agricultural tradition. Where tall prairie grass once stood, miles of corn and soybeans now poke out of the level surface. This region has its share of small cities as well. Springfield, Decatur, and Bloomington-Normal all have populations of over 80,000. Springfield, of course, is the capital of Illinois and home to the Governor's Mansion, Abraham Lincoln's tomb, and a rich political history that dates back to before the Civil War. The counties along the Illinois River have an even older history. Greene County in particular boasts a number of majestic mansions from the bygone era of large steamboats and cattle ranches. Heartlanders are generally salt of the earth folks.

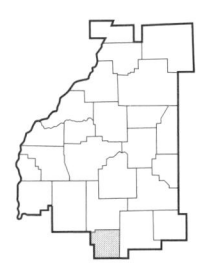

Bond County

Population: 18,055
County Seat: Greenville
Total Area: 383 square miles
Per capita income: $17,947
Year Established: 1817

Burgess Township

James Nolan Home

During the early 1880s, local residents gathered nightly around an abandoned farmhouse outside the small town of Pocahontas in order to catch a glimpse of strange lights that emanated from within. Some claimed to hear sounds and even see the ghost of a man leaving the house with the body of a headless woman cradled in his arms. One skeptical reporter blamed the lights on a prankster.

Source: "A Haunted Farmhouse," *Daily Republican* (Decatur) 20 June 1883; Clark, Jerome. *Unnatural Phenomena: A Guide to the Bizarre Wonders of North America* (Santa Barbara: ABC-CLIO, 2005).

The Nolan farm was located somewhere two miles southwest of Pocahontas.

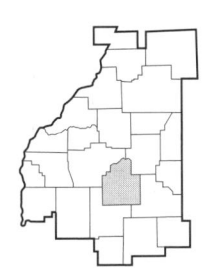

Christian County

Population: 35,372
County Seat: Taylorville
Total Area: 716 square miles
Per capita income: $17,937
Year Established: 1839

CLARKSDALE

Anderson Cemetery

"Cemetery X" or "Graveyard X," as it is known, is actually Thomas Anderson Cemetery, located south of Taylorville near the tiny town of Clarksdale. It was founded in 1867 by Tavner and Polly Anderson. This cemetery's claim to fame seems to be its inclusion in a documentary called "America's Most Haunted," which Troy Taylor highly dramatized in *Beyond the Grave* as well as *Confessions of a Ghost Hunter*. Dozens of amateur pictures of mists and orbs taken here have circulated the Internet. According to local legend, there is a phantom wolf that guards the cemetery and an old section that is only reachable at night after "the trees part." Attempts to keep this graveyard's identity a secret may have inadvertently attracted more attention to this location.

Source: Taylor, Troy. *Beyond the Grave: The History of America's Most Haunted Graveyards*. Alton: Whitechapel Productions Press, 2001; Kleen, Michael. "Cemetery X." *Legends and Lore of Illinois* 1 (July 2007): 1-6.

Thomas Anderson Cemetery is located off E. 990N Road, just west of the unincorporated community of Clarkdale. The cemetery closes at dusk.

Robber's Court

For many years, a small stone cabin with a long, brick chimney stood along the road near a bridge, not too far from Anderson Cemetery. It was rumored to be guarded by a zombie dog and to be the home of a family of murdering thieves. Inside, the cabin was always warm, no matter how cold it was outside. A girl—or a witch—was said to have been hung from the steel bridge past the

112 | *Michael Kleen*

cabin. Spook lights are sometimes seen floating around the creek under the bridge. The cabin has since been relocated.

Source: http://theshadowlands.net/places/illinois.htm.

The stone cabin no longer exists, but the bridge can be found along 900N, just west of Clarkdale and south of Thomas Anderson Cemetery.

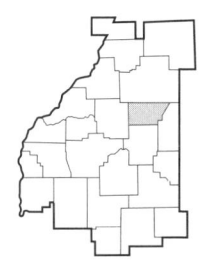

DeWitt County

Population: 16,798
County Seat: Clinton
Total Area: 405 square miles
Per capita income: $20,488
Year Established: 1839

Tunbridge Township

Old Union Cemetery

Old Union Church was established 10 miles west of Clinton on October 13, 1831, near a large, white oak tree. The preacher at the church was a man named Hugh Bowles. That church only remained open for fifty years because its attendees moved to Clinton when the railroad was built. A second church, which had a seating capacity of 600, was erected in 1864 in front of the cemetery. "Springs of never failing water" flowed from the foot of the hill on which the new building sat.

Troy Taylor maintains that two cemetery workers and a sheriff's deputy told him that visitors have seen "glowing balls of light" in the graveyard at night. A private plot near the back of the cemetery, which is surrounded by an ornate fence and contains a single monument, has been accused of giving visitors "bad vibes."

Haunting Illinois: The Heartland

Source: Kleen, Michael. "Old Union Cemetery." *Legends and Lore of Illinois* 2 (October 2008): 1-8; Taylor, Troy. *Weird Illinois: Your Travel Guide to Illinois' Local Legends and Best Kept Secrets*. New York: Sterling Publishing, 2005.

Old Union Cemetery is located down a dirt road off of 200E, northwest of Route 54 and north of Salt Creek. The cemetery closes at dusk.

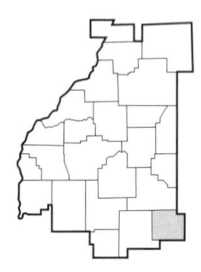

Effingham County

Population: 34,264
County Seat: Effingham
Total Area: 480 square miles
Per capita income: $18,301
Year Established: 1831

Effingham

Ramsey Cemetery

Haunted "Caves" (rock shelters) are Ramsey Cemetery's claim to fame. Formed by thousands of years of erosion, generations of local residents have carved their names, alongside proclamations of love, into the sandstone walls. Legend has it that a werewolf and a man with glowing red eyes inhabit the area. According to several histories of Effingham County, the backcountry was always rough and tumble, and the roads and hills were inhabited by transients and brigands. Some of them may have occupied the rock shelters near Ramsey Cemetery. As for the cemetery itself, it is rumored to be haunted by a man who committed suicide there in a chapel that has since been torn down. That story, at least, is true. The unfortunate incident occurred in the spring of 1961. Since the publication of the *Legends and Lore of Illinois* issue on Ramsey Cemetery,

114 | *Michael Kleen*

relatives of the victim informed me that his name was Ottis. Distraught over his wife's infidelity, he blocked the entrance to the cemetery with his car and shot himself with a shotgun.

Source: Kleen, Michael. "Ramsey Cemetery." *Legends and Lore of Illinois* 3 (February 2009): 1-8; Lewis, Chad and Terry Fisk. *The Illinois Road Guide to Haunted Locations*. Eau Claire: Unexplained Research Publishing, 2007.

Ramsey Cemetery is located north of Effingham at the end of County Road 1230E, on the west side of the Little Wabash River. The cemetery closes at dusk.

Saint Anthony's Hospital Fire

St. Anthony's Hospital opened on September 15, 1877. Its mission, as established by the Hospital Sisters of Saint Francis, was to care for the sick and the poor in rural Illinois. The white habits of the Franciscan nuns were a welcome sight in the community. Tragically, at midnight on April 4, 1949, a fire ravaged the hospital. "Neighbors awakened by screams and the tinkling crash of breaking windows ran out to stare into a nightmare," *Time* magazine reported. Between 74 and 77 people, including ten newborn babies, were killed out of the 116 patients and ten staff. Fern Riley, a 22-year-old nurse, refused to leave the nursery and died alongside the newborns. The superintendent of St. Anthony's, Frank Ries, also perished when he ran back into the burning building to try and rescue his wife. The hospital was rebuilt in 1952, but the heroism of the hospital staff and Effingham firefighters will always be remembered.

Source: "Sorrow in the 'Heart of the U.S.'." *Life Magazine*, 18 April 1949, 29-33; "Illinois: Glare in the Sky." *Time Magazine*, 18 April 1949; St. Anthony's Memorial Hospital. *A Tradition of Caring Since 1875*. Effingham: St. Anthony's Memorial Hospital, 2004 (http://www.st anthonyshospital.org/PDF/ historybook.pdf).

St. Anthony's Memorial Hospital is located at 503 North Maple Street in Effingham. www.stanthonyshospital.org

Haunting Illinois: The Heartland | 115

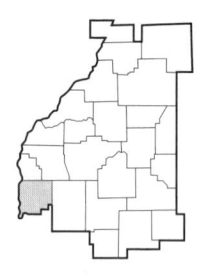

Greene County

Population: 14,761
County Seat: Carrollton
Total Area: 546 square miles
Per capita income: $15,246
Year Established: 1821

Eldred

J. Eldred Home

The James J. Eldred home is a grand, Greek-Revival ranch house that has stood abandoned since the 1930s. During the 1860s and '70s, James and his wife Emeline had a reputation for hosting grand parties at their "Bluff Dale Farm," but life was harsh living along the Illinois River. The three Eldred daughters, Alma, Alice, and Eva, all died of illness at home in their beds. Both Alice and Eva were 17. Alma was only four years old. In 1999, the home was listed on the National Register of Historic Places, and in recent years the Illinois Valley Cultural Heritage Association has made great strides in restoring it to its former glory. While there are no specific ghost stories about the property, its current owners list "phantom footsteps," "phantom knocking at the front door," "giggles of a young lady," and "small shadows moving in the nursery" as phenomenon experienced there.

Source: http://www.eldredhouse.com.

The J. Eldred Home is located along 1300N, near the intersection of 1300N and River Road, just north of Eldred. This home is privately owned.

Walkerville Township

The Sweetin Home

Otherwise known as "the old stone house," the remnants of this manor were, at one time, part of a mansion built in 1848 by a stockman named Azariah Sweetin. Though nothing but a shell today, a grand ballroom once occupied the third floor, a ballroom that was the scene of murder. During a

116 | *Michael Kleen*

farewell gala for newly enlisted Union soldiers, two farmhands, Henson and Isham, got into an argument that ended with one thrusting a knife into the back of the other. The wounded man fell down by the fireplace and bled to death. According to legend, his blood seeped into the stone floor and formed an outline of his body. The stain could never be removed.

As the war raged, Azariah Sweetin didn't want to take any chances, so he stuffed all his gold coins into jars and buried them around his property. Unfortunately, an equestrian accident in 1871 rendered him without any memory of where he had buried his money. After his death, his ranch was purchased by Cyrus Hartwell, who also lived there until he died. Treasure seekers soon tore the mansion apart, but no one has ever found Azariah's gold. Storytellers say Azariah's ghost—alongside snakes—now guards his lost loot.

Source: Henson, Michael Paul. *A Guide to Treasure in Illinois and Indiana*. Dona Ana: Carson Enterprises, 1982; Taylor, Troy. *Weird Illinois: Your Travel Guide to Illinois' Local Legends and Best Kept Secrets*. New York: Sterling Publishing, 2005; http://www.accessivcha.com/index_files/Scenic BluffRoad.htm.

The ruins of the Sweetin Home are located near the intersection of River Road and 430E, just north of Apple Creek.

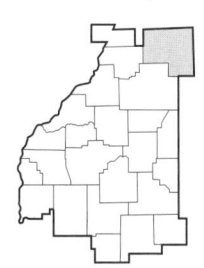

LIVINGSTON COUNTY

Population: 39,678
County Seat: Pontiac
Total Area: 1,045 square miles
Per capita income: $18,347
Year Established: 1837

CHATSWORTH

1887 Chatsworth Train Wreck

At around midnight on the hot summer night of August 10, 1887, a train full of 700 passengers bound for Niagara Falls crossed a partially burnt bridge, causing it to collapse. The first engine made it across safely, but the trestle collapsed under the second. This caused a chain reaction in which

Haunting Illinois: The Heartland

the six wooden passenger cars cascaded into each other. The *Chicago Times* reported, "The groans of men and the screams of women united to make an appalling sound, and above all could be heard the agonizing cries of little children as in some instances they lay pinned alongside their dead parents." Many of the passengers were saved because the rear sleeper cars stopped before they reached the wreckage, but unfortunately nearly 85 passengers were killed and between 169 and 372 were injured. It was one of the worst train wrecks in United States history. It was thought that the trestle collapsed because of a controlled burn that had not been properly extinguished.

Source: "1887 Train Wreck Near Chatsworth One of Worst in U.S.," *The Pantagraph* (Bloomington) 5 August 2007; http://www.peoria countyillinois .Info/news/chatsworthacc.html.

The train wreck occurred three miles east of Chatsworth, between Chatsworth and Piper City. The railroad tracks run slightly north of Route 24.

STREATOR

Moon Point Cemetery

Moon Point Cemetery is an old graveyard located just south of Streator in Livingston County. Like other rural graveyards, it became an object of folklore in the late 1960s and '70s when local teens, looking for a place to 'hang out' after dark, picked this isolated location to drink, spin yarns, and play pranks on one another. Moon's Point got its name from Jacob Moon who, along with his daughter and three sons, was the first to settle the area. Locals believe the cemetery is haunted by the ghost of a "hatchet lady." This lady went insane, the story goes, after either her son or daughter died, and every full moon, her spirit is seen stalking the cemetery, hatchet in hand.

Another tale associated with Moon Point concerns an abandoned house—previously owned by a witch, of course—that is also rumored to be haunted. Many tales of séances and illicit trespasses have come from that location. The remoteness of the cemetery is accentuated by the fact that a railroad track bisects the road leading to it. It is said that anyone who is caught in the cemetery while a train passes will be trapped there. That much is true. According to legend, however, your car will also die and not be able to restart until after the train has gone.

Source: Kleen, Michael. "Moon Point Cemetery." *Legends and Lore of Illinois* 3 (May 2009): 1-8; "Moon Creek legend ripe for Halloween," *Times-Press* (Streator) 28 October 2001.

Moon Point Cemetery is located just south of Streator, down a gravel drive off 3150N, west of Route 23 and the railroad tracks. The cemetery closes at dusk.

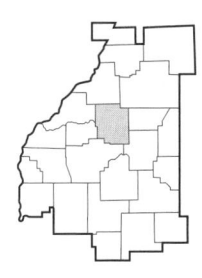

LOGAN COUNTY

Population: 31,183
County Seat: Lincoln
Total Area: 619 square miles
Per capita income: $17,953
Year Established: 1839

ELKHART

Elkhart Cemetery

Elkhart Cemetery is the resting place of Governor Richard Oglesby, who lived in the town of Elkhart for many years before his death. "Elkhart" actually comes from "Elk Heart Hill," the name given to the area by the Illini Indians. A village of Kickapoo occupied the hill until the early 1800s. To this day, locals claim that the ghosts of American Indians can be seen in and around the cemetery. Another legend associated with Elkhart is that there are trails in the woods behind the graveyard, and if you venture down the wrong one, you will never return. Some visitors have reported seeing the ghost of Governor Oglesby's wife mourning in front of their mausoleum.

Haunting Illinois: The Heartland

Source: Lewis, Chad and Terry Fisk. *The Illinois Road Guide to Haunted Locations*. Eau Claire: Unexplained Research Publishing, 2007.

Elkhart Cemetery is located just west of Elkhart and Interstate 55, off 700th Street. The cemetery closes at dusk.

LINCOLN

Lincoln College

Lincoln College is a private, two year residential school established in 1865 by the Cumberland Presbyterian Church. It was named after then President Abraham Lincoln, just a few weeks before he was assassinated. Its Lincoln campus has about 700 students. Two buildings are said to be haunted. The first, University Hall, was built in 1866. Students have seen a face appear in the bell tower and white shadows in the windows. Others report hearing footsteps when they were in the building alone. These apparitions belong to two students, a boy and girl, who allegedly died in the late 1800s. Olin Sang Hall is thought to be the haunt of a prankster ghost who unplugs electronics and shuts doors.

Source: http://theshadowlands.net/places/illinois.htm; http://ww w.lincolncollege.edu/lynxonline/w06/Steven%20Hall.pdf.

Lincoln College is located at 300 Keokuk Street in Lincoln.

NEW HOLLAND

400th Avenue Bridge

The 400th Avenue bridge crosses Sugar Creek just north of Pool Hill Cemetery. According to local lore, the area is a supernatural hotspot and was the scene of lynching in the distant past. Visitors occasionally hear whispering, talking, rattling chains, and screams as if the lynchings were being repeated over and over again. Even the nearby fields are not immune from this macabre auditory replay. Also, if you lay your hand on the tree where the hangings occurred, it is said that you will witness the events.

Source: http://theshadowlands.net/places/illinois.htm.

The 400th Avenue bridge is located along 400th Avenue, just south of Route 10.

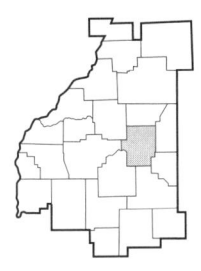

MACON COUNTY

Population: 114,706
County Seat: Decatur
Total Area: 585 square miles
Per capita income: $20,067
Year Established: 1829

DECATUR

Avon Theater

One of Decatur's many historic theaters, the Avon Theater opened in 1916 and predominantly catered to the new motion picture craze. Its interior was the largest and most elaborately decorated in Decatur. Renovations and a brief closure in the 1950s removed most of its glamour, however, and by 1986 it was abandoned. Luckily, in the mid-1990s, a group of entrepreneurs purchased the theater and again opened it for business. After its re-opening, the staff began to experience strange events that included hearing laughter, footsteps, and applause after hours. Items would also appear and disappear. Staff members have also seen the apparition of Gus Constan, who owned the Avon during the 1960s. Theater patrons have also described feeling as though they were pushed or had bumped into something unseen.

Source: Taylor, Troy. *Flickering Images: The History & Hauntings of the Avon Theater.* Alton: Whitechapel Productions Press, 2001.

The Avon Theater is located at 426 North Water Street, one block south of Route 36. The theater is open during regular business hours. www.theavon.com.

Haunting Illinois: The Heartland | 121

Greenwood Cemetery

Greenwood Cemetery is rumored to be one of the most haunted locations in central Illinois. According to Troy Taylor, the land that would become Greenwood was originally an Amerindian burial ground and then was later used by the first white settlers to bury their dead until the late 1830s. These graves have since disappeared. The oldest visible marker on the grounds dates back to 1840, and Greenwood Cemetery was officially established in 1857.

One of the most interesting stories at Greenwood concerns the ghosts of dead and dying Confederate prisoners who were dumped at the cemetery on their way to a prison camp and buried in the hillside under what is now a memorial to Union soldiers. Years later, heavy rain collapsed part of the hill, mixing the bodies together. The hill was repaired and the bodies reburied, but many believe their spirits were permanently disturbed. Another popular legend concerns the so-called "Greenwood Bride," who wanders the grounds in her wedding dress searching for her fiancé, who was murdered by bootleggers. Greenwood Cemetery is also haunted by phantom funerals, ghost lights that flicker in the southeastern hills, and other, more sinister apparitions.

Source: Kleen, Michael. "Greenwood Cemetery." *Legends and Lore of Illinois* 1 (February 2007): 1-6; Taylor, Troy. *Where the Dead Walk: History & Hauntings of Greenwood Cemetery.* Alton: Whitechapel Productions Press, 2002.

Greenwood Cemetery is located at the end of Church Street, north of Lincoln Park Drive and west of Route 51 in Decatur. The cemetery closes at dusk.

Millikin University

Millikin University began its career with great fanfare. Named after the man who bankrolled the school, James Millikin, it opened in 1903 and was dedicated by Teddy Roosevelt. Classes began on September 15 of that year. Its numerous ghost stories have their origins early on in its history. One story, involving the light of a long-deceased railroad crossing watchman named Tommy, has been told on campus since the 1930s. The old gymnasium, now used primarily as a storage area, is the scene of echoes from days gone by. According to Troy Taylor, students have heard the sounds of sports being played while alone in the abandoned gym. Aston Hall, formerly an all-female dorm, is reportedly haunted by the ghost of a young woman who committed suicide there in the 1940s. She roams the third floor, and only her upper body is visible.

Source: Taylor, Troy. *Ghosts of Millikin: The History & Hauntings of Millikin University*. Alton: Whitechapel Productions Press, 2001.

Millikin University is located at 1184 West Main Street between Route 48 and N. Oakland Avenue. www.millikin.edu.

OAKLEY TOWNSHIP

Peck Cemetery

Peck Cemetery is of the typical rural stock, formerly hidden in a wood at the end of a gravel road. Today, houses dot the pothole-filled road, the gravel path to the cemetery is now a driveway, and "Beware of dogs" and "no trespassing" signs are prominently displayed. Hidden from view prior to the 1990s, Peck Cemetery was the perfect place to hold nighttime excursions far from any prying eyes. The evidence of these excursions included burnt candles, graffiti, and headless statues covered in red paint. It was rumored that the leader of a Satanic cult installed a "devil's chair" in the cemetery, on which he would sit during rituals. If anyone else sat on the chair, they would die within a year. Troy Taylor lists "inexplicable cries," "whispers and voices," "hooded figures," "eerie lights," and "the sound of a woman's scream" as other phenomenon experienced at this cemetery.

Haunting Illinois: The Heartland | 123

Source: Kleen, Michael. "Peck Cemetery." *Legends and Lore of Illinois 2* (August 2008): 1-7; Taylor, Troy. *Haunted Decatur Revisited: Ghostly Tales from the Haunted Heart of Illinois.* Alton: Whitechapel Productions Press, 2000.

Peck Cemetery is located off Donavan Road, just south of the Sangamon River and west of Route 32. The cemetery closes at dusk.

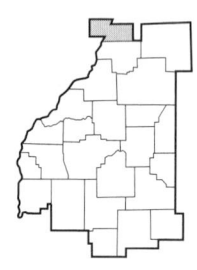

MARSHALL COUNTY

Population: 13,180
County Seat: Lacon
Total Area: 399 square miles
Per capita income: $19,065
Year Established: 1839

EVANS TOWNSHIP

Cumberland Cemetery

Cumberland Cemetery is said to be the home of a headless lady, spook lights, and the ghost of a little girl. The cemetery itself is rich in history. It was the site of the first farm in Evans Township, and its rolling hills were once occupied by a fort built during the Black Hawk War to protect the nearby settlers from marauding Sauk, Fox, and Kickapoo Indians. The main ghost story associated with the cemetery involves a headless woman. There is no evidence to substantiate the story, but that has not stopped its proliferation. According to legend, a farmer began to suspect his wife was having an affair with one of the young men who hung around his farm looking for work. Crazed with jealousy, he cornered his wife in their barn and confronted her. Despite her pleas and denials, the farmer took his ax and chopped off her head. From then on, her ghost stalked the cemetery, searching for her missing head.

124 | *Michael Kleen*

Source: Kleen, Michael. "Cumberland Cemetery." *Legends and Lore of Illinois* 3 (August 2009): 1-8; Lewis, Chad and Terry Fisk. *The Illinois Road Guide to Haunted Locations*. Eau Claire: Unexplained Research Publishing, 2007.

Cumberland Cemetery is located off Cumberland Road along Sandy Creek, about four miles northwest of Wenona. The cemetery closes at dusk.

LAWN RIDGE

Lost Copper Coin/Medallion

In August 1870, three men drilling an artesian well discovered a small copper coin or medallion more than 100 feet beneath layers of clay and soil. The profile of a woman holding a child and wearing a headdress was crudely etched onto one side, and a figure with ears like a mule or rabbit was etched into the other. Strange writing or symbols appeared around the edges of the coin. The coin found its way to the Smithsonian and generated much discussion among coin-experts, geologists, and archeologists. The coin or medallion showed signs of age, but its origins were mysterious. Some speculated that a French or Spanish explorer dropped it in a deep hole as a practical joke. Others believed it was a hoax perpetrated by the men who drilled the well. Incredibly, a third theory maintains that the coin or medallion was evidence of an ancient, lost civilization in North America.

Source: Clark, Jerome. *Unnatural Phenomena: A Guide to the Bizarre Wonders of North America* (Santa Barbara: ABC-CLIO, 2005); http://www.badarchaeology.net/data/ooparts/peoria.php.

Lawn Ridge is a small community along Route 40 at the border between Marshall and Peoria counties.

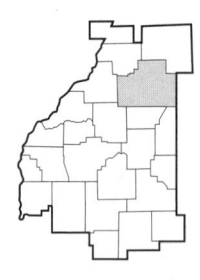

McLean County

Population: 150,433
County Seat: Bloomington
Total Area: 1,186 square miles
Per capita income: $22,227
Year Established: 1830

Normal

Illinois State University

Founded in 1857 and originally a teacher's college, Illinois State University is currently home to around 23,000 students and faculty, as well as one tenacious ghost. The ghost is said to be that of Angeline V. Milner, or Ange for short, a beloved librarian who remained with her books long after she passed from this world. In 1917, the university moved its library from the Old Main Building to North Hall, where Miss Milner worked until she died. North Hall served as the library until 1940, when a new building was constructed and christened "Milner Library" to honor Normal University's beloved Aunt Ange. In 1976, the old Milner Library became known as Williams Hall, and most of the university's books were moved into the new Milner Library, located on the north side of campus. Since at least the 1980s, staff members working in the Williams Hall archives have reported encounters with what they believe is the ghost of Ange Milner, still tending to her books. These books have recently been moved again, to a brand new storage facility. Has Ange Milner's ghost followed her books to their new location, or has she finally found peace? Only time will tell.

Source: Kleen, Michael. *Paranormal Illinois*. Atglen: Schiffer Publishing, 2010; Christensen, Jo-Anne. *Ghost Stories of Illinois*. Edmonton: Lone Pine, 2000.

Illinois State University is located at 100 N. University Street, just east of Route 51, between Normal and Bloomington.

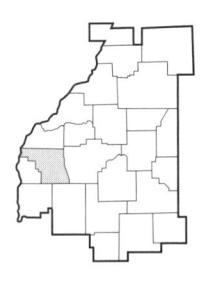

Morgan County

Population: 36,616
County Seat: Jacksonville
Total Area: 572 square miles
Per capita income: $18,205
Year Established: 1823

Jacksonville

Illinois College

Founded by Presbyterians in 1829, Illinois College is one of the oldest colleges in Illinois. Its first president was Edward Beecher, brother of Henry Ward Beecher and Harriet Beecher Stowe. With such a rich history, it comes as no surprise that Illinois College is rich in ghostlore too. Nearly every building on campus is thought to have a ghost or two. Like Millikin University, the female dorm at Illinois College, Ellis Hall, is haunted by a young woman who allegedly committed suicide there. A "gray ghost"—a faceless phantom at that—hangs out on the stairwell of Whipple Hall. Another gray ghost, this one dressed in a Confederate uniform from the Civil War, has been seen in Sturtevant Hall. Phantom footsteps have been heard in Beecher Hall, the oldest building on campus. It is rumored that early in the college's history, medical students stole cadavers from nearby hospitals in order to learn about anatomy. After a while, the hall where the bodies were stored began to smell, and the students' grisly enterprise was uncovered.

Source: Brooks-Posadas, Rachel. *Ghosts of Springfield and Southern Illinois*. Atglen: Schiffer Publishing, 2009.

Illinois College is located at 1101 West College Avenue, just north of Route 67 and 104 (Morton Avenue) in Jacksonville. www.ic.edu.

Haunting Illinois: The Heartland | 127

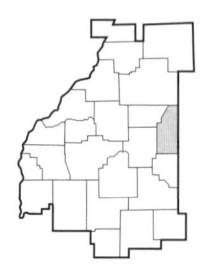

PIATT COUNTY

Population: 16,493
County Seat: Monticello
Total Area: 440 square miles
Per capita income: $21,075
Year Established: 1841

UNITY TOWNSHIP

Payroll Payload

Many years ago, in the early 1800s, there was an old army way station in southern Piatt County near Arthur. It was well known in the area that several companies of regular army soldiers were coming there to receive their monthly pay, which meant that a total of around $286,000 in $20 gold coins was at the station. A gang of bandits planned to rob the station before the soldiers arrived. The station master learned of their plans, however, and with the help of several guards, he buried the gold coins. When the bandits arrived, they killed the station master and his guards and burnt the station to the ground. However, they never found the $286,000 in gold, which is presumably still buried somewhere nearby.

Source: Henson, Michael Paul. *A Guide to Treasure in Illinois and Indiana.* Dona Ana: Carson Enterprises, 1982.

The way station referred to in this story may be known today as Pierson Station, which is located between Atwood and Hammond just off Route 26.

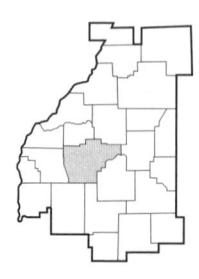

SANGAMON COUNTY

Population: 188,951
County Seat: Springfield
Total Area: 877 square miles
Per capita income: $23,173
Year Established: 1821

New Berlin

Charles Kinney Home

Late in April 1893, an associate of wealthy stockman W.B. Smith shot and killed himself in his home, where Smith had been storing some furniture. Soon after the man's death, his neighbors reported hearing strange noises in the house. Smith's creditors became suspicious that he was removing his furniture during the night, so they sent two men to watch it. The men observed a light in the house accompanied by a voice, so they climbed up a ladder to get a look in the second floor. To their surprise, they saw Charles Kinney, the man who had committed suicide weeks earlier, sitting on the bed. The phantom reenacted his suicide and then disappeared. The two men gathered some neighbors together, and they searched the house but found no evidence of a hoax.

Source: "A Ghost Story," *Daily Republican* (Decatur) 10 May 1893; Clark, Jerome. *Unnatural Phenomena: A Guide to the Bizarre Wonders of North America* (Santa Barbara: ABC-CLIO, 2005).

New Berlin is located southwest of Springfield along Old Route 54, just south of Interstate 72.

Springfield

Dana-Thomas Home

In 1902, Susan Lawrence Dana hired renowned architect Frank Lloyd Wright to remodel a home she had recently purchased. The renovations cost a total of $60,000, and when they were completed, Susan owned arguably the most unique home in Springfield. She lived there between 1904 and 1928. During that time, she was very active in the Spiritualist Movement and held séances there. Since it opened as a museum, employees and volunteers working in the home have reported some unusual experiences. In one instance, Mike Anderson, a musician who has performed at the home for several decades, felt the temperature drop suddenly for several minutes. Volunteer coordinator Kathy Liesman told the *State Journal-Register* that she had heard humming, the sound of chairs tumbling down the stairs, and has even seen a lady dressed in black wandering the home when no tour groups were present.

Source: "Dana-Thomas House's Creepy Tales Revealed," *State Journal-Register* (Springfield) 24 October 2009; Brooks-Posadas, Rachel. *Ghosts of Springfield and Southern Illinois*. Atglen: Schiffer Publishing, 2009.

The Dana-Thomas home is located at 301 E. Lawrence Ave. in Springfield. It is open 9am to 4pm Wednesday through Sunday. www.dana-thomas.org

Sober Duck/Brewhouse (Former)

On June 27, 1968, a bartender at the Sober Duck Disco and Rock Club named Albert Cranor committed suicide with a gunshot to the head. During life, his friends and coworkers called him "Rudy." After his death, they blamed icy chills during the summer and flying shot glasses on his ghost. One waitress claimed a disembodied head appeared and warned her of the club owner's impending death. The owner of the building died soon after. Tom Blasko, who had leased the building for his club, asked two priests to perform an exorcism. In August 1979, they said the rites inside the Sober Duck, and the disturbances stopped. The club's name was later changed to the Brewhouse, and it burnt down under mysterious circumstances in 1992 after having been abandoned for over three years.

Source: Scott, Beth and Michael Norman. *Haunted Heartland: True Ghost Stories from the American Midwest*. New York: Barnes & Noble Books, 1985, 1992; Taylor, Troy. *Haunted Illinois: The Travel Guide to the History & Hauntings of the Prairie State*. Alton: Whitechapel Productions Press, 2004.

The Sobor Duck/Brewhouse was formerly located at 2840 Fox Bridge Road, but that address is now an empty lot.

Yates Mansion

Richard Yates Sr. was Governor of Illinois between the tumultuous years of 1861 and 1865, when the country was torn apart by Civil War. With half the state being for the war and half against, Yates—a Republican—sometimes found himself at odds with his own citizens.

Contrary to some reports, however, Richard Yates Sr. did not build this house. This mansion was built in 1905, while Richard Yates Sr. died in 1873. This mansion was owned and occupied by his son, Richard Yates Jr., who was also Governor of Illinois (1901-1905). Some residents of the mansion say he never left. The ex-governor is said to haunt a small room in the tower of the mansion, where he kept his books and Civil War memorabilia. His footsteps can still be heard, pacing across the floor.

Source: Taylor, Troy. *Haunted Illinois: The Travel Guide to the History & Hauntings of the Prairie State*. Alton: Whitechapel Productions Press, 2004; http://en.wikipedia.org/wiki/Richard_Yates,_Jr.

The Yates Mansion is located at 1190 Williams Blvd, on the east end of Washington Park. This is a private residence.

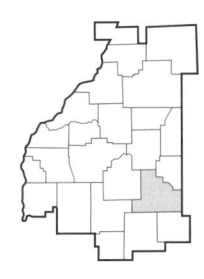

SHELBY COUNTY

Population: 22,893
County Seat: Shelbyville
Total Area: 768 square miles
Per capita income: $17,313
Year Established: 1827

COLD SPRING TOWNSHIP

Williamsburg Hill

Ridge Cemetery and Williamsburg Hill are notorious in the lore of central Illinois. The hill is the highest point in Shelby County and once sheltered a town, in addition to its cemetery. Williamsburg, as the town was known, was platted in 1839 by two men, Thomas Williams and William Horsman. Many Horsmans can be found buried in Ridge Cemetery to this very day. The town disappeared in the 1880s as the railroad bypassed its inconvenient location. The legends surrounding Ridge Cemetery involve occult rituals, spook lights, phantom funerals, and the ghost of an old man who disappears upon approach. Animal mutilations have also been reported in and around the cemetery.

Source: Kleen, Michael. "Ridge Cemetery." *Legends and Lore of Illinois 1* (September 2007): 1-6; Taylor, Troy. *Haunted Decatur Revisited: Ghostly Tales from the Haunted Heart of Illinois*. Alton: Whitechapel Productions Press, 2000.

Ridge Cemetery and Williamsburg Hill are located at the end of 1100E, several miles south of Tower Hill. The cemetery closes at dusk.

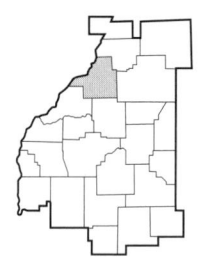

TAZEWELL COUNTY

Population: 128,485
County Seat: Pekin
Total Area: 658 square miles
Per capita income: $21,511
Year Established: 1827

CREVE COEUR

Cole Hollow Road Monster

Stories of bigfoot and other mythic creatures are not often associated with Illinois; however, in the 1970s the Illinois River Valley was abuzz with sightings of the Cole Hollow Road Monster, or Cohomo, for short. It was first sighted along Cole Hollow Road, just outside of Creve Coeur south of Peoria. It was described as a three-toed beast, eight to ten feet tall, with a coat of thick white fur. There were so many sightings in the summer of 1972 that the Tazewell County Sheriff's Department organized a search party to hunt for the creature. Encounters with Cohomo tapered off after that, but one man believed he caught a glimpse of it in the headlights of his car one night in July 2000, farther north up the Illinois River near Essex, Illinois.

Source: Taylor, Troy. *Weird Illinois: Your Travel Guide to Illinois' Local Legends and Best Kept Secrets*. New York: Sterling Publishing, 2005.

Coles Hollow Road begins off E. Washington Street in East Peoria and runs south for several miles, past Interstate 474, until it ends at Route 98.

East-Central Illinois

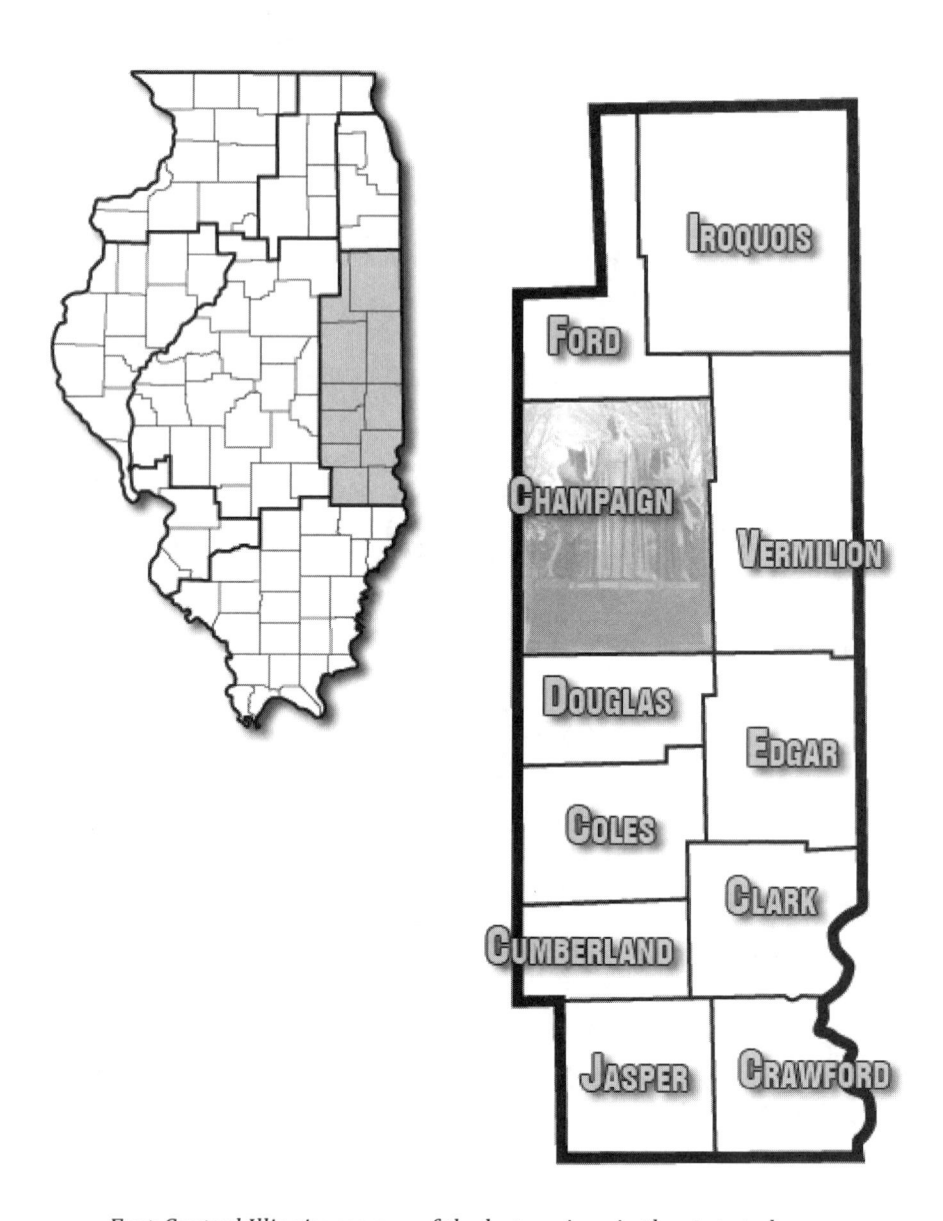

East-Central Illinois was one of the last regions in the state to be settled. Passed over in favor of better land, the pioneers considered this area along the Embarras and Vermillion rivers to be a wilderness wasteland filled with Indians, snakes, and wolves. In time, however, the land was tamed here too. The region is now home to two of the state's universities: the University of Illinois in Champaign and Eastern Illinois University in Charleston. For such a small region, this area is home to quite a few ghost stories, including one of the most famous: Pemberton Hall's Mary Hawkins.

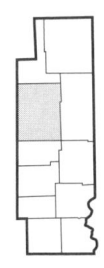

Champaign County

Population: 179,669
County Seat: Urbana
Total Area: 998 square miles
Per capita income: $19,708
Year Established: 1833

CHAMPAIGN

University of Illinois

The University of Illinois was established as an industrial university in 1867 and first opened on March 2, 1868. It became the University of Illinois in 1885 and was renamed the University of Illinois at Urbana-Champaign in 1982. As the oldest public university in the state of Illinois, the campus hosts a number of ghost stories. The English Building is purportedly haunted by the ghost of a student who either drowned or committed suicide there in the early 1900s during the time when the building served as a female dormitory. The third floor of Lincoln Hall has its own ghost, but so does the ultra-modern Psychology Building, where a student threatened to kill himself by jumping from one of the upper floors overlooking the foyer. He survived the incident unscathed but died a few years later. Some students claim that his ghost has returned to torment his analytically-minded former classmates. Even the YMCA cannot claim to be ghost-free. According to legend, the spectral manifestation of Chief Illiniwek is said to roam the basement of this venerable building, which formerly hosted a painting of the university's mascot. Perhaps all the recent controversy has contributed to his unrest!

Source: Taylor, Troy. *Haunted Illinois: The Travel Guide to the History & Hauntings of the Prairie State.* Alton: Whitechapel Productions Press, 2004; Thuma,

Haunting Illinois: East Central Illinois | 135

Cynthia and Catherine Lower. *Creepy Colleges and Haunted Universities*. Atglen: Schiffer Publishing, 2003; http://the 217.com/articles/view/cu_buildings_boast_ spirits_ghosts_and_ghouls.

The University of Illinois is located between the sister cities of Champaign and Urbana. The Illini Union, at the heart of campus, is located at 1401 W. Green Street. The YMCA building is located at 1001 S. Wright Street.

CRITTENDEN TOWNSHIP

Giant Snake

On June 6, 1896, a farmer named Carl Smithson discovered a giant snake (about 18 feet in length) in his barn. It was in the process of swallowing the leg of his Jersey calf. Evidently the snake, which had been spotted by several other farmers, fled before Smithson could return with help. A posse was formed to search for the creature, but it is unknown whether they succeeded.

Source: "Illinois Boasts a Snake Story," *Daily Republican* (Decatur) 12 June 1896; Clark, Jerome. *Unnatural Phenomena: A Guide to the Bizarre Wonders of North America* (Santa Barbara: ABC-CLIO, 2005).

This giant snake was last seen seven miles southeast of Tolono.

RANTOUL

Chanute Air Force Base

Chanute Air Force Base opened in Rantoul in July 1917 and was a vital part of the local economy for nearly 76 years. After its closure in 1993, much of the base was divided up into residential and commercial properties, but most of the core buildings remain abandoned. Inevitably, local kids exploring the abandoned parts of the base in the past few years have begun to bring home unusual stories. Some visitors have, through the broken windows, reported seeing an officer working at his desk. Others say they have seen phantom airmen strolling the weed-choked sidewalks or sitting in the cockpits of the planes behind the Air Museum. On September 13, 2001, at 10PM, a police K-9 unit responded to a trespassing call at White Hall, one of the largest abandoned buildings on base. Dutch, an experienced canine with 957 drug arrests under his collar, pursued something up to the roof, where he suddenly and unexpectedly leapt 15 feet off the building and fell to his death.

Source: Kleen, Michael. "Chanute Air Force Base." *Legends and Lore of Illinois* 3 (June 2009): 1-8; http://petmemorialcards.com /mem2001-13.html.

The remains of Chanute Air Force Base are located on the south side of Rantoul, and the Chanute Air Museum is located at 1011 Pacesetter Drive, inside a former hanger. The base's campus is open to visitors, but the buildings are not.

URBANA

Clements Cemetery

Clements Cemetery, at the hinterlands of Champaign-Urbana, is home to a ghost known as the Blue Man. In the early 1840s, passersby discovered the body of a man hanging from a tree near the cemetery. They cut him down and buried him in an unmarked grave. While that story is generally believed to explain the presence of the Blue Man, a family named Blue also lived in the area, perhaps lending their surname to the phantom. Blue Man is supposed to appear in the cemetery, glowing bright blue, in the advent of each full moon.

Source: Taylor, Troy. *Haunted Illinois: The Travel Guide to the History & Hauntings of the Prairie State*. Alton: Whitechapel Productions Press, 2004.

Clements Cemetery is located northeast of Urbana along High Cross Road, past Interstate 74, between 1800N and E Oaks Road.

Urbana High School

Built in 1914 and designed in the Tudor style, Urbana High School has undergone repeated renovations in the past 96 years. One of those renovations inadvertently gave birth to a ghost story that has endured at the school for several generations. Between 1914 and 1986, a small area known as "the Tower" was home to two classrooms, one for art and one for music. The Tower is located in the central portion of the school and was accessed by a narrow set of stairs. During the renovations of the 1980s, the tower was closed because it couldn't be made accessible to handicapped students.

Students at the high school have their own explanation for the closing, however. They believe the Tower was locked up after a love affair between a teacher and a student ended in tragedy. The teacher reportedly hung herself from the indoor fire escape. According to Troy Taylor, the door to the Tower is said to open without cause, and lights can be seen in the windows at night. Once, when staff members called police to investigate whether someone was trespassing in the Tower, they heard loud, unexplainable tapping.

Source: Taylor, Troy. *Haunted Illinois: The Travel Guide to the History & Hauntings of the Prairie State*. Alton: Whitechapel Productions Press, 2004; http://www.usd116.org/uhs/UHS_history/features/tower.htm.

Urbana High School is located at 1002 S. Race Street, just south of the intersection of Race and Iowa Street. The school is not open to the general public.

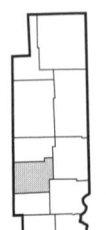

COLES COUNTY

Population: 53,196
County Seat: Charleston
Total Area: 510 square miles
Per capita income: $17,370
Year Established: 1831

Ashmore

Ashmore Estates

The building now known as Ashmore Estates began as part of the Coles County Poor Farm. It was built after the State Board of Charities condemned the first almshouse on that farm for its poor conditions. The cornerstone of the new "fireproof" building was laid on May 17, 1916. Coles County sold its almshouse to Ashmore Estates, Inc. in February 1959, and that company opened it as a private psychiatric hospital. In the early 1980s, the building was used as a home for the mentally and developmentally disabled. Ashmore Estates finally closed its doors in 1987. In the summer of 2006, Scott and Tanya Kelley purchased the building and opened it as a haunted attraction. Over the years, many strange stories have been told about Ashmore Estates, including rumors that a patient murdered his fellow inmates with an axe and that the nurses abandoned their wards inside the building. Some employees working there during the 1980s witnessed figures walking around at night after all the rooms had been locked. In June 2008, Ursula Bielski and Edward L. Shanahan brought twenty people on an overnight stay at Ashmore Estates as part of a series of events known as "Beyond the Veil."

Source: Kleen, Michael. *Paranormal Illinois*. Atglen: Schiffer Publishing, 2010; Kleen, Michael. "Ashmore Estates." *Legends and Lore of Illinois* 3 (September 2009): 1-8; "Investigators Say Ashmore Estates is Haunted," *Coles County Leader* (Tuscola), 27 October 2006.

Ashmore Estates is located off Route 16 along 1050N, about 1.2 miles west of Ashmore. Ashmore Estates is only open during scheduled events.

St. Omer Cemetery

St. Omer Cemetery is home to an unusual family monument that some say looks like a crystal ball on top a pyre. According to local lore, Caroline Barnes, one of four people buried under the massive stone, was put to death for practicing witchcraft. It is said that no pictures can be taken of her monument and that it glows on moonless nights. The only evidence for the legend seems to be the gravestone's dramatic design, the way local citizens grow nervous whenever the story is mentioned, and most strikingly, Caroline's impossible date of death chiseled in the granite: February 31. The monument also faces north and south, while most headstones are oriented east-west. There is no historical or documentary evidence supporting the notion that Caroline Barnes was accused of witchcraft, but nevertheless, the legend has persisted.

Source: Kleen, Michael. "St. Omer Cemetery." *Legends and Lore of Coles County, Illinois* 1, no. 3 (2006); Lewis, Chad and Terry Fisk. *The Illinois Road Guide to Haunted Locations*. Eau Claire: Unexplained Research Publishing, 2007; "Witch's Grave in Coles County?" *Coles County Leader* (Tuscola), 31 October 2003.

St. Omer Cemetery is located at the end of a narrow gravel drive off N. Oakland Road (2400N), about 1.5 miles north of Ashmore.

CHARLESTON

Pemberton Hall

Pemberton Hall is the oldest all-female dormitory in the state of Illinois and was the brainchild of Livingston C. Lord, president of Eastern Illinois University from 1899 to 1933. The old-English look and feel of the dormitory was well suited for its first full time matron, Mary Hawkins, who emigrated from Great Britain in 1901 and assumed the position of dorm director in August 1910 when she was 33 years old. Sometime after her death, the girls of Pemberton began to believe her ghost returned to haunt the hall. The Roommate's Death, a common folklore motif in which a student is murdered by a crazed junitor, has merged with the story of Mary Hawkins to create a unique tale. Sometimes Mary manifests herself as a prankster, a young woman who scratches at doors, leaves bloody footprints, or wanders up to the fourth floor dressed in nothing but a white gown. Other times, Mary appears as a benevolent matriarch who makes sure doors are locked at night and warns "her girls" of trouble.

Source: Kleen, Michael. *The Legend of Pemberton Hall*. Charleston: Black Oak Press, Illinois, 2008; Scott, Beth and Michael Norman. *Haunted Heartland: True Ghost Stories from the American Midwest*. New York: Barnes & Noble Books, 1985, 1992.

Pemberton Hall is located at the corner of Route 16 (Lincoln Avenue) and 4th Street on the campus of Eastern Illinois University.

Tycer Home

Dennis F. Hanks, a cousin of Abraham Lincoln, once owned this 157-year-old home, and during the 1960s and '70s it was widely reputed to be haunted by his ghost. In 1965, Marie and Forster [Forrester] Tycer purchased the house, renovated it, and turned it into a museum. Mr. Tycer told the *Eastern News* that he was doing some electrical work in the basement when he lost his balance and almost fell into the wiring. He claimed that unseen hands pushed him away and saved his life.

Mrs. Tycer saw the reflection of the ghost in a mirror or window as she was painting the porch. She turned around, but found that she was alone. She also heard footsteps and claimed the ghost unlocked doors. In 1970, Mrs. Tycer committed suicide with a gunshot to the head in an upstairs bedroom. According to legend, the bloodstains continued to reappear no matter how many times they were scrubbed away. The next family to live in the home occupied it for quite some time and never experienced anything out of the ordinary.

Source: "Haunted House in Charleston?" *Eastern News* (17 July 1968); "Ghosts roam local haunts…" *Eastern News* (28 October 1977).

The Tycer home is located at 218 Jackson Avenue in Charleston. This is a private residence.

MATTOON

"Ragdoll" Cemetery

The quaint and unassuming Bethel Cemetery sits nestled among rolling hills and picturesque farms south of the Coles County Airport. According to legend, there was once a little girl of about eight or nine years of age who was very attached to her rag doll. The girl died tragically, some say of an illness, others say murder. In the case of the illness, she asked to be buried with her doll, but when the time came, the doll was nowhere to be found. To this day, the doll forever searches for the girl's grave. In the other version of the story, the doll was buried with the girl and crawls out of the grave every night to look for her killer. It is also said to be seen hanging from the oak tree by her grave and will attack anyone who dares to come near.

Source: Kleen, Michael. "Bethel (Rag Doll) Cemetery." *Legends and Lore of Coles County, Illinois* 1, no. 7 (2006); "Twisted Tales," *Times-Courier* (Charleston) 23 October 2007.

Bethel Cemetery is located at the juncture of 600N and 1020E, just south of the Coles County Airport.

MORGAN TOWNSHIP

Airtight Bridge

Designed by Claude L. James and built in 1914, Airtight Bridge spans the narrow Embarras River in rural Coles County and was long known as a drinking spot and a hangout for rough characters. That all changed on the pleasant Sunday morning of October 19, 1980. According to newspaper reports, two men from rural Urbana spotted the body of a nude woman about 50 feet from the bridge as they drove past. The body was missing its head, hands, and feet. After an extensive murder investigation, no killer was ever located and the identity of the victim remained a mystery for years. Ever since then, an aura of mystery has surrounded the bridge. Locals say it earned the name "Airtight" because of the unnatural stillness encountered while crossing it, or because early automobiles would stall on the steep hill leading to the bridge if there was more air than gas in their fuel tank. The bridge is currently closed to traffic.

Source: Kleen, Michael. *Paranormal Illinois*. Atglen: Schiffer Publishing, 2010; Kleen, Michael. "Airtight Bridge." *Legends and Lore of Coles County, Illinois* 1, no. 1 (2006); "Some believe ghosts roam the bridge," *News-Gazette* (Champaign) 31 October 2005.

Airtight Bridge is located along Airtight Road (2130E), a few miles northeast of Charleston.

CUMBERLAND COUNTY

Population: 11,253
County Seat: Toledo
Total Area: 347 square miles
Per capita income: $16,953
Year Established: 1843

UNION TOWNSHIP

A Giant Skeleton & Lost Treasure

In 1920, two reddish-colored skeletons were unearthed in a gravel bank on a farm owned by a man named Jake Walters in rural Cumberland County. One was giant sized—twice as large as the other adult skeleton. The lower jaw of the giant was well preserved with ten teeth that were worn down, indicating that he or she died at an old age. The bones were buried four feet below the surface in a region of prehistoric trails and burial grounds at the extreme end of a ridge east of Hurricane Creek. The ridge was already well known for its tales of buried treasure. According to legend, a young Indian Chief, most likely of the Kickapoo, told the white settlers that

Haunting Illinois: East Central Illinois | 143

an elder of the tribe had buried a treasure there, but he would not reveal its location because anyone who dug it up would be cursed and die. About the time the giant skeleton was found, a fortune teller in Charleston claimed to know where the treasure was buried but "will not tell until the right person to claim it comes along."

Source: The Cumberland County Historical and Genealogical Societies of Illinois. *Cumberland County History*. Olney: Taylor Print Shop, 1968.

The giant skeleton was found on private property two miles north of Union Center, on the east side of Hurricane Creek.

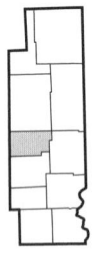

Douglas County

Population: 19,922
County Seat: Tuscola
Total Area: 417 square miles
Per capita income: $18,474
Year Established: 1859

Chesterville

Chesterville Cemetery

Chesterville is a small Amish and Mennonite community that consists of no more than a few dozen houses located a couple of miles away from Rockome Gardens. Within the neatly trimmed grounds of Chesterville Cemetery, an old oak tree stands at the edge of the woods that separates the graveyard from the river. The peculiar thing about this tree is the iron fence that surrounds it and the old stone marker that no longer bears a name. According to Troy Taylor, this is the grave of a woman who turned up dead after being accused of witchcraft in the early 1900s after she challenged the

144 | *Michael Kleen*

conservative views of the local Amish church elders. The town planted a tree over her grave to trap her spirit inside and prevent her from taking revenge. Her ghost can still be seen from time to time hanging around the area.

Source: Lewis, Chad and Terry Fisk. *The Illinois Road Guide to Haunted Locations.* Eau Claire: Unexplained Research Publishing, 2007; Kleen, Michael. "Chesterville Cemetery." *Legends and Lore of Illinois* 1 (April 2007): 1-5; Taylor, Troy. *Haunted Decatur Revisited: Ghostly Tales from the Haunted Heart of Illinois.* Alton: Whitechapel Productions Press, 2000.

Chesterville Cemetery is located off County Road 450E, north of Route 133, on the east bank of the Kaskaskia River.

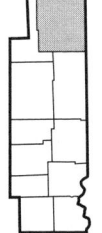

IROQUOIS COUNTY

Population: 31,334
County Seat: Watseka
Total Area: 1,118 square miles
Per capita income: $18,435
Year Established: 1833

WATSEKA

The Watseka Wonder

One of the most compelling cases of spirit possession in American history occurred right here in Illinois. In 1878 in the small town of Watseka, a 13-year-old girl named Lurancy Vennum began to slip into short-lived comas. When she awoke, she spoke of having gone to heaven and claimed to have communicated with spirits. Her parents sought the help of Dr. E. Winchester Stevens, who was a doctor and a spiritualist. Dr. Stevens advised Lurancy to allow one of the spirits to take over her body until she was strong enough to fight the catatonic spells on her own. Lurancy complied, and when she awoke, she claimed to be Mary Roff, who died in a mental hospital when Lurancy was an infant. Incredibly, Mary Roff's family still lived in Watseka, and Lurancy asked to be returned to them. As "Mary Roff," she seemed to have intimate knowledge of her former life and convinced the Roffs that she was indeed channeling the soul of their long-deceased daughter. After four months, she said it was time to depart, and Lurancy awoke with no knowledge of what had happened. To this day, no one has been able to explain this incredible event.

Source: Christensen, Jo-Anne. *Ghost Stories of Illinois*. Edmonton: Lone Pine, 2000; Scott, Beth and Michael Norman. *Haunted Heartland: True Ghost Stories from the American Midwest*. New York: Barnes & Noble Books, 1985, 1992.

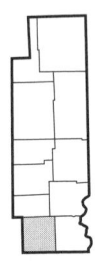

JASPER COUNTY

Population: 10,117
County Seat: Newton
Total Area: 498 square miles
Per capita income: $16,649
Year Established: 1831

FALMOUTH

Love Ford Bridge

The area around Love Ford Bridge is home to several notorious places, not the least of which is Happy Holler, a bar and sound stage popular with bikers, truckers, and hunters. Just across the road, at the top of a hill derogatively named after the African Americans thought to be buried there, sits Higgins (Coburn) Cemetery. Strange lights and sounds have been encountered near the cemetery, and it is rumored to be the site of animal sacrifice and Devil worship. Love Ford Bridge is believed to be haunted by the ghost of an inebriated young man who jumped into the Embarras River and drowned.

Source: Lewis, Chad and Terry Fisk. *The Illinois Road Guide to Haunted Locations*. Eau Claire: Unexplained Research Publishing, 2007.

Love Ford Bridge and Higgins (Coburn) Cemetery are located along E. 1400th Avenue, which can be accessed off Route 130, several miles north of Newton.

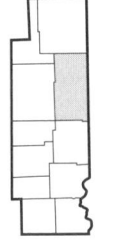

VERMILION COUNTY

Population: 80,067
County Seat: Danville
Total Area: 902 square miles
Per capita income: $16,787
Year Established: 1826

DANVILLE

Fischer Theatre

The Fischer Theatre was originally known as the Grand Opera House, which was built in 1884 and opened on November 5, 1884. The theater was built on the site of the former home of a Danville physician named W.W.R. Woodbury and played its first motion picture in 1889. In 1912, Louis F. Fischer purchased a controlling interest in the opera company and remodeled the building. Several businesses occupied the floors above the theater. It closed in 1982, and a preservation effort was launched.

In 2004, the Vermilion Heritage Foundation asked the Springfield Ghost Society to investigate the theater after a volunteer accidentally recorded clicks, bangs, and dragging sounds in the projection booth when he left his recording equipment on overnight. The group experienced some phenomenon during their investigation including "dark colored shadows" and "a dark figure," but the ghosts failed to materialize during a haunted tour conducted in 2005.

Source: "Paranormal Activity Slow During Tours," *News-Gazette* (Champaign) 31 October 2005; http://www.fischertheatre.com/his tory.asp; http://www.springfieldghostsociety.com/sgs/Investigations/ Fischer/fischer_theatre.html.

The Fischer Theatre is located at 158 N Vermilion St. at the corner of Vermilion and Harrison. It is open during special events only. www.fischertheatre.com

Haunting Illinois: East Central Illinois | 147

Metro-East

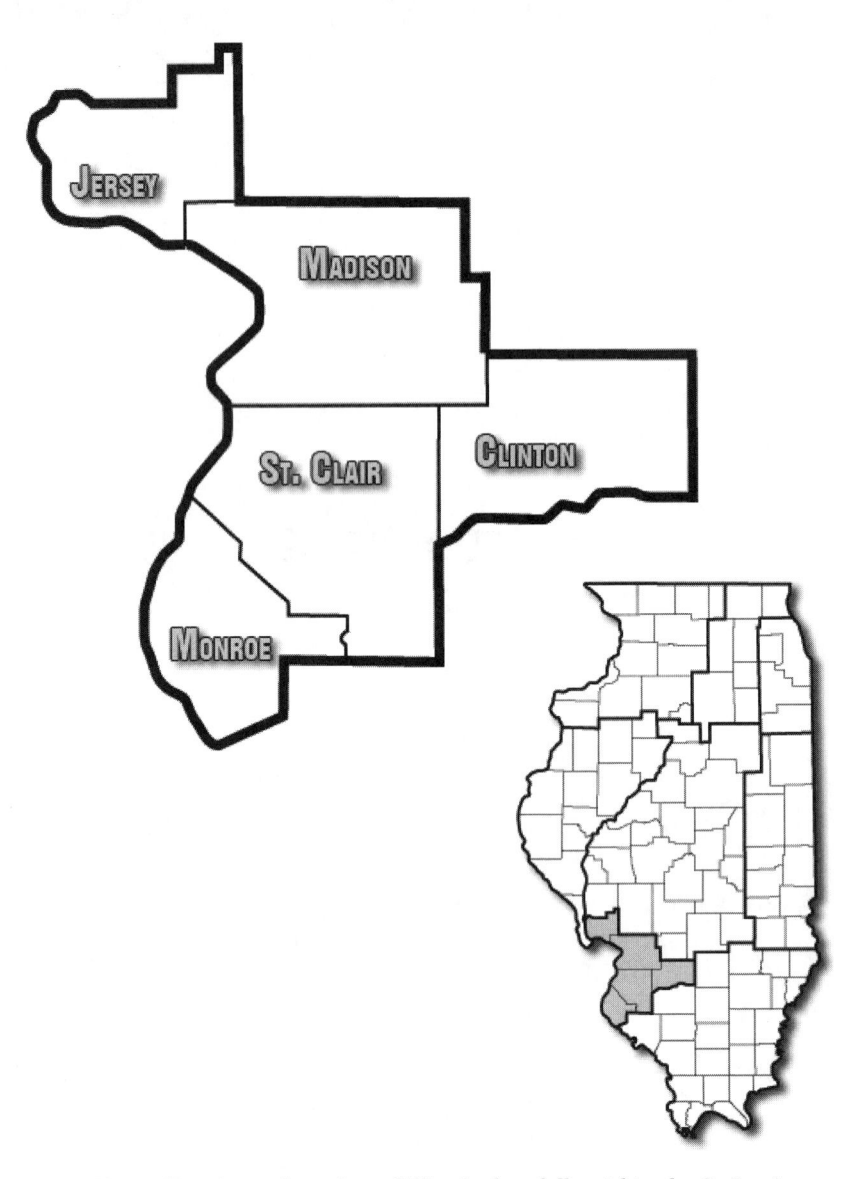

Metro-East is a sub-region of Illinois that falls within the St. Louis Metropolitan Area, and as a result, residents here are much more likely to root for the St. Louis Cardinals than for the Chicago Cubs. This region is also the commercial center of central and southern Illinois. For hundreds of miles around, consumers flock to Fairview Heights to patronize its malls and shopping centers. With its position at the juncture of the Illinois and Mississippi rivers, the Metro-East region is steeped in history and has always been culturally diverse. It was at the heart of the Mississippian culture for hundreds of years, and its early European settlers were predominantly French.

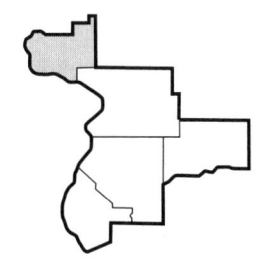

Jersey County

Population: 21,668
County Seat: Jerseyville
Total Area: 377 square miles
Per capita income: $19,581
Year Established: 1839

Grafton

Ruebel Hotel

The Ruebel Hotel has survived the test of time and has seen the best and worst the Illinois and Mississippi rivers have to offer. It is named after its original owner, Michael Ruebel, who opened the austere, brick hotel in 1884. After one hundred years of serving the miners and river workers of Grafton, it was abandoned. Its clientele had long dried up. In 1997, new owners acquired the Ruebel Hotel and opened it for business once again. The new staff quickly discovered that one guest—a young girl named Abigail—had never left. Her ghost has been spotted roaming the hallway, but no one knows who she was or why she might haunt the building.

Source: Kachuba, John B. *Ghosthunting Illinois*. Cincinnati: Clerisy Press, 2005; Taylor, Troy. *Haunted Alton: History & Hauntings of the Riverbend Region*. Alton: Whitechapel Productions Press, 1999.

The Ruebel Hotel is located at 217 E. Main Street (Route 100) in downtown Grafton. It is open during regular business hours. www.ruebelhotel.com.

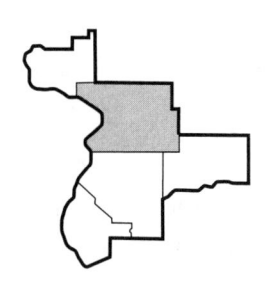

Madison County

Population: 258,941
County Seat: Edwardsville
Total Area: 740 square miles
Per capita income: $20,509
Year Established: 1812

ALTON

McPike Mansion

Built in 1869 by Henry Guest McPike and designed in the Italianate-Victorian style, this mansion has long captured the imaginations of Alton residents. Although it was added to the National Register of Historic Places in 1980, it has sat abandoned for decades—attracting vandals and the curious alike. Ghost stories were told about the mansion even when it was occupied. In the 1940s, boarders often heard children running up and down the stairs but could find no one when they investigated the noise. After the mansion became derelict, passersby reported seeing faces in the windows. There are two known entities here. The mansion's new owners named one of them Sarah. She is thought to have been a hired hand in life and teases visitors with a spectral touch or hug. The other ghost belongs to a former owner, Paul Laichinger. He has been spotted wandering the grounds.

Source: Lewis, Chad and Terry Fisk. *The Illinois Road Guide to Haunted Locations*. Eau Claire: Unexplained Research Publishing, 2007; Taylor, Troy. *Haunted Alton: History & Hauntings of the Riverbend Region*. Alton: Whitechapel Productions Press, 1999.

The McPike Mansion is located at 2018 Alby Street, at the corner of Alby and E. 20th Street. This is a private residence. www.mcpikemansion.com.

Spirits Lounge

In 2006, Gary Graham and Tim Brueggeman purchased this old Masonic temple and planned to open it as a bar, restaurant, and banquet center. The two made extensive renovations, knowing the building already had a reputation for being haunted. Unusual occurrences happened almost immediately upon its grand opening in 2007. Built around 1900, the Piasa Lodge of the Freemasons occupied the building for nearly a century. According to Gary Hawkins, who placed the former lodge on his ghost tour, it is occupied by dozens of ghosts, including two master Masons named James Brown and Frank Harris, a woman named Mrs. Smalley who haunts the lady's lounge, and two children. Four Confederate soldiers who died of smallpox are also believed to haunt one of the former temple's two basements, which were all that remained of an older building over which the Piasa Lodge was built.

Source: "Friendly Spirits: Bar Hosts Weddings, Receptions – and Possibly Ghosts," *The Telegraph* (Alton) 14 January 2009; http://www.templeentertainmentinc.com/Pages/Stories.html.

The Temple Banquet Center and Spirits Lounge is located at 300 State Street in Alton and is open during regular business hours. www.templeentertainmentinc.com

COLLINSVILLE

Lebanon Road

On or around Lebanon Road are seven railroad bridges, some no longer in use. All of them are heavily coated in graffiti—a testament to their popularity for nighttime excursions. Local visitors have crafted a hellish tale around these seven bridges, which they dubbed the "Seven Gates to Hell." The legend is that if someone were to drive through all seven bridges and enter the last one exactly at midnight, he or she would be transported to Hell. In some versions, the person entering the final tunnel must be a skeptic. In other versions, no tunnel can be driven through twice in order for the magic to work. Like Cuba Road in Barrington, an abandoned property near Lebanon Road has given rise to rumors of a "death house." A closed road or driveway is alleged to lead to an old house in which a family was murdered. Moreover, a group of Satanists are said to sacrifice animals and children at the location.

Source: Kleen, Michael. "Lebanon Road." *Legends and Lore of Illinois* 3 (January 2009): 1-8; Lewis, Chad and Terry Fisk. *The Illinois Road Guide to Haunted Locations*. Eau Claire: Unexplained Research Publishing, 2007.

The "haunted" section of Lebanon Road begins at Spring Avenue on the west side of Collinsville and runs to Longhi Road. Not all the bridges are along Lebanon Road. Some are along Lockmann Road. Follow the railroad tracks on a map of the area.

Haunting Illinois: Metro-East | 153

East Alton

Old Milton School

Most recently home to a decorative glass company, from 1904 to 1984 this building served as Milton Elementary School. Locals whisper that during the 1930s, a dark event left a stain on the history of the school. According to legend, a janitor raped and murdered a girl in the gym locker room. Suspicion fell on the janitor after he failed to report to work the next day. Not long after, he returned to the school and took his own life. Since that time, female visitors have experienced very negative feelings in that area of the building, even if they have never heard the story. Up until the school closed in 1984, one educator in particular reported seeing and hearing the ghost of a young girl in her office. Others encountered a more hostile spirit—that of the murderous janitor. A psychic reportedly exorcized this negative presence. Milton School appeared in an episode of SyFy Channel's *Ghost Hunters* on October 6, 2010.

Source: "Alton Paranormal Hotspot to be Featured on 'Ghost Hunters'," *The Telegraph* (Alton) 25 September 2010; Taylor, Troy. *Haunted Alton: History & Hauntings of the Riverbend Region*. Alton: Whitechapel Productions Press, 1999.

The former Milton School building is located along Milton Road, between Fernwood and Edgewood avenues. This is private property.

Godfrey

Lewis & Clark College

First opened in 1838 as Monticello Female Seminary, Lewis & Clark College is widely believed to be haunted by the ghost of Harriet Haskell, who guided the institution with a steady hand for four decades. Even when in 1888 a fire devastated campus, Miss Haskell raised the money necessary to rebuild the school. It became known as Lewis & Clark College in 1971. Students and educators alike maintain that Harriet Haskell has remained at her college, protecting and watching over the institution. Some students have even encountered her in the hallways. Furniture has been known to move on its own. Haskell's ghost is most frequently seen in the library, which was her favorite place in life.

Source: Jo-Anne. *Ghost Stories of Illinois*. Edmonton: Lone Pine, 2000; Taylor, Troy. *Haunted Alton: History & Hauntings of the Riverbend Region*. Alton: Whitechapel Productions Press, 1999.

Lewis & Clark Community College is located at 5800 Godfrey Road (Route 67 and 111) in Godfrey. www.lc.edu.

HARTFORD

Hartford Castle

"Hartford Castle" is the colloquial name for a mansion that formerly stood on a tract of land just outside of Hartford, Illinois, across the river from St. Louis. The mansion's actual name was Lakeview, but few besides the original owner referred to it as such. The original owner was a French immigrant named Benjamin Biszant, who built the imposing home for his bride, an Englishwoman whose name has apparently been lost to history. Eventually, Biszant's wife died and, perhaps, the pain was too much for him to remain at Lakeview. He sold the mansion and moved west. A number of owners and tenants occupied the estate until the last owners abandoned it in the 1960s. In 1972, vandals destroyed the interior, and a fire ravaged the grounds a short time later. Today, the Hartford Castle is nothing more than a hole in the ground, surrounded by concrete debris and a shallow moat. Several of the original gazebos remain behind.

Source: "Elegant Reminder of the Past Is Destroyed," *Lewis & Clark Journal* 25 March 1973; Kleen, Michael. "Hartford Castle." *Legends and Lore of Illinois* 2 (November 2008): 1-7; Taylor, Troy. *Haunted Illinois: The Travel Guide to the History & Hauntings of the Prairie State*. Alton: Whitechapel Productions Press, 2004.

The ruins of the Hartford Castle are located in a wooded area off New Poag Road, east of Route 3 and south of Hartford, just east of the railroad tracks. This is private property.

Haunting Illinois: Metro-East

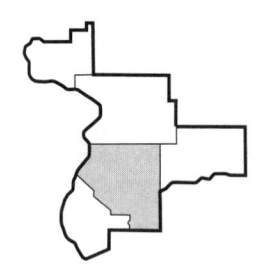

St. Clair County

Population: 256,082
County Seat: Belleville
Total Area: 674 square miles
Per capita income: $18,932
Year Established: 1790

Belleville

Jakob Meyer Home

Jakob Meyer, a coal miner of German descent, built this impressive brick home and lived there until the ripe old age of 77, when he ended his own life in his parlor. The house was quiet for the next four decades, until 1962. By that time, Judy and Dollie Walta had opened a music school there and taught lessons undisturbed for six years, until the untimely death of a friend at sea. Their friend's return, in the form of phantom footsteps and visitations, apparently disturbed the eternal rest of Jakob Meyer. Judy and Dollie Walta began to smell cigar smoke and see a large man in the parlor, a man who was not their former friend. They looked into the history of the house and uncovered the story of Meyer's suicide. Manifestations have tapered off since then, but a whiff of Meyer's cigar still occasionally wafts through the empty parlor.

Source: Anderson, Jean. *The Haunting of America*. Boston: Houghton Mifflin, 1973; Hauck, Dennis William. *Haunted Places: The National Directory: Ghostly Abodes, Sacred Sites, UFO Landings, and Other Supernatural Locations*. New York: Penguin Books, 1994, 1996.

The Jakob Meyer home is located at the corner of Main and 17th streets. This is a private residence.

Ritz Theater

Bloomer Amusement Corporation opened the Ritz Theater in 1929, offering cheap ticket prices for motion picture fans. Janitors working at the theater experienced strange things over its 60 years in operation. During the 1970s, one employee heard a woman's voice calling for help, saw lights flash on and off, and also found his radio smashed to pieces even though he was the only person in the building. Others have seen the curtain shake or witnessed the shadow of a man standing behind the curtain. A number of these events occurred in 1971 when the balcony was sealed off to create a separate auditorium. The ghost is thought to be that of a man who once worked at the theater, who may have been upset at the changes. The Ritz Theater building is now the home of Faith Baptist Church.

Source: Taylor, Troy. *Haunted Alton: History & Hauntings of the Riverbend Region*. Alton: Whitechapel Productions Press, 1999; http://cinema treasures.org/theater/1858/.

The Ritz Theater was located in the northeast corner of N. Charles and E. Main streets in downtown Belleville. This is private property.

COLLINSVILLE

Cahokia Mounds

Cahokia Mounds State Historic Site consists of dozens of prehistoric mounds constructed by American Indians around the time that Leif Ericson's longships landed in Vinland. The most prominent feature of these mounds is Monk's Mound. Monk's Mound was the largest earthen structure north of central Mexico at the time of its construction. The mounds were a part of a large city, which reached the height of its power between 1000 and 1200 AD. A wooden stockade, which the residents rebuilt several times, surrounded the central structures at the site, although there is no evidence of battles or who their enemy might have been. A nearby structure, known as "woodhenge," suggests this civilization had knowledge of astronomy. At the time the first French explorers began to penetrate the Illinois territory, the native peoples had no knowledge of who had once occupied the massive site.

Source: Emerson, Thomas and Barry Lewis. *Cahokia and the Hinterlands: Middle Mississipian Cultures of the Midwest.* Urbana, Illinois: University of Illinois Press, 1991; Kleen, Michael. "Cahokia Mounds." *Legends and Lore of Illinois 2* (December 2008): 1-7.

Cahokia Mounds State Historic Site is located at 30 Ramey Street, off Collinsville Road, just south of Interstate 55/70. www.cahokiamounds.org.

Lebanon

McKendree University

Founded in 1828 by the United Methodist Church and originally known as Lebanon Seminary, McKendree University is the oldest college in the State of Illinois. Like most colleges, several places on campus are rumored to be haunted. The Alumni House is stalked by three restless spirits: that of an old lady, her husband, and an infant. The old nursery where the infant died is said to be much colder than the rest of the house. Bothwell Chapel, one of the oldest buildings on campus, seems to have attracted the most attention. A former security guard claims to have heard organ or piano music playing in the sanctuary after hours. According to legend, a student hung himself in the bell tower, and to this day his ghost can be heard pacing the upper floors. Carnegie Hall has less specific hauntings. Students report odd feelings and electronic devices that exhibit unusual behavior, such as a television turning on or changing channels on its own.

Source: http://theshadowlands.net/places/illinois.htm.

McKendree University is located at 701 College Road in northwestern Lebanon, east of Locust Hills Golf Course. www.mckendree.edu.

Tapestry Room

The building currently occupied by the Tapestry Room Restaurant was built around 1850, and some locals believe it may have served as a stop on the Underground Railroad because of a tunnel that leads to its basement and connects several local businesses. Shortly before Gwen and Bob Barcum opened their restaurant for business, an electrician working in the far corner of the basement was frightened by the appearance of a pair of spectral legs ascending the staircase. During a paranormal investigation in 2003, Len Adams and his team claimed to have heard a thunderous bang or knock on the wall in response to one of their questions. A former cook, who lived in an apartment at the rear of the building, frequently heard the sound of furniture being tossed around the restaurant at night. The next morning, everything would be in its proper place.

Source: Adams, Len. *Phantoms in the Looking Glass: History and Hauntings of the Illinois Prairie*. Decatur: Whitechapel Press, 2008.

The Tapestry Room is located at 127 W. Saint Louis Street in Lebanon and is open during regular business hours. www.thetapestryroom.com

FREEBURG TOWNSHIP

The Albino Tracks

Also known simply as "the Ghost Tracks," this abandoned rail line is home to a very monochrome legend. Some locals maintain that in the 1800s, shortly after the railroad was laid, an epidemic tore through the nearby farming community, and the superstitious farmers blamed it on a pair of albino twins that had been born a few years before. They abducted the children and tied them to the railroad tracks, where the two were struck and killed by a train. As in the Crybaby Bridge legend, the ghosts of the albino children are said to push stalled vehicles over the railroad tracks to prevent a similar fate. Another version of the story has a local family being struck by a train after their wagon became stuck at the crossing. Today, the tracks have been removed, but the ghosts still roam the area.

Haunting Illinois: Metro-East

Source: Lewis, Chad and Terry Fisk. *The Illinois Road Guide to Haunted Locations*. Eau Claire: Unexplained Research Publishing, 2007; Taylor, Troy. *Weird Illinois: Your Travel Guide to Illinois' Local Legends and Best Kept Secrets*. New York: Sterling Publishing, 2005.

The "Albino Tracks" were located just south of Belleville and Mascoutah along Rentchler Road, between Reinneck and Jefferson roads.

Little Egypt

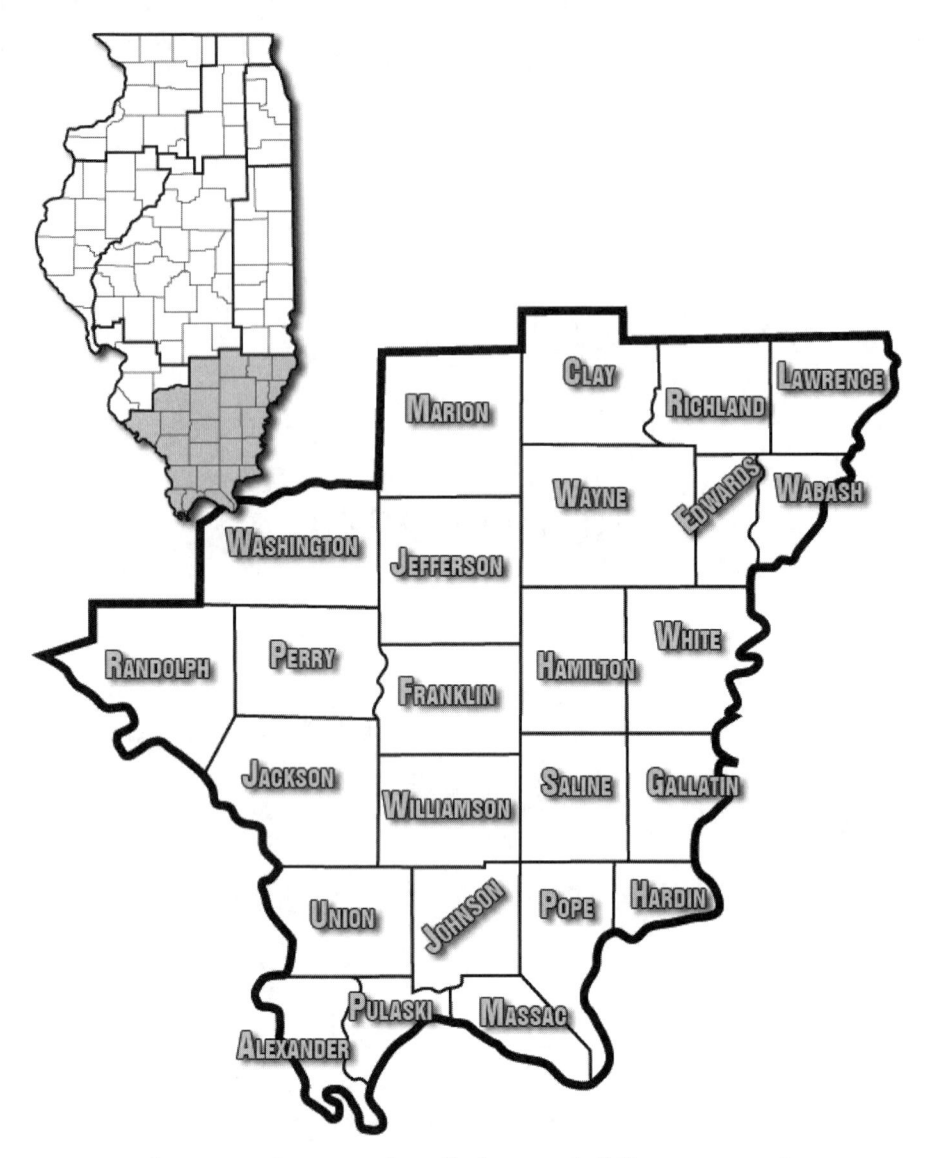

Little Egypt is the most culturally distinct of all Illinois regions. It is known as "Little Egypt" because of its proximity to a vital river trade route (like the Nile delta in Egypt) and the presence of towns with names like Cairo, Thebes, Dongola, and Karnak. The early settlers of the region were all from Southern states like Virginia, North Carolina, and Tennessee. Slavery existed here until the 1850s, and many residents sympathized with the Confederacy during the Civil War. Today, Little Egypt has a dwindling population as mining and manufacturing jobs moved out of the area. Carbondale, home of SIU, is considered the unofficial capital of Southern Illinois.

Franklin County

Population: 39,018
County Seat: Benton
Total Area: 431 square miles
Per capita income: $15,407
Year Established: 1818

Buckner

Harrison Cemetery

One of the oldest graveyards in Franklin County, Harrison Cemetery is said to be home to two luminous phantoms. The "male" spirit appears with an orange glow in a nearby field. The "female" spirit is white in hue and is usually seen near the back of the cemetery. The far corner is also the home of a third legend, that of a piano that plays at midnight. This legend is clearly tied to an unusual looking headstone set apart from the others. With its oversized piano keys, it appears to memorialize a child, perhaps one with an interest in music, but there is no name or date to give any clues as to whom it belonged. Although not officially chartered until 1907, Harrison Cemetery has served area residents for over 120 years and is named after one of the first families to settle Browning Township.

Source: Kleen, Michael. "Harrison Cemetery." *Legends and Lore of Illinois* 3 (November 2009): 1-8.

Harrison Cemetery is located at the intersection of Washington Street and Harrison Road between the towns of Christopher and Buckner. The cemetery closes at dusk.

Haunting Illinois: Little Egypt | 163

Gallatin County

Population: 6,445
County Seat: Shawneetown
Total Area: 328 square miles
Per capita income: $15,575
Year Established: 1812

Equality

Hickory Hill Plantation

Also known as the Crenshaw House or the Old Slave House, this mansion was built in 1838 by John Crenshaw and his brother Abraham. Crenshaw owned vast salt mines in Southern Illinois and was one of the wealthiest men in the entire state. He also owned over 740 slaves. Illinois entered the Union in 1818 with strict "black codes" on the books. The Illinois constitution prohibited the slave trade but permitted those residents already holding slaves to keep their property. Visitors to Crenshaw's plantation included Abraham Lincoln. Slaves were kept in cramped cells in the attic of the mansion.

As early as 1851, there were reports that the mansion was haunted. The German family who operated the estate between 1850 and 1864 reported hearing strange sounds coming from the attic. After the Civil War and the abolition of slavery, tourists began to come and visit Illinois' only plantation. They heard phantom footsteps, voices, and singing. A legend spread that no one could spend the night in the attic. Many tried, but every last one was scared off before dawn. In the late 1920s, one "ghost hunter" is believed to have died after spending the night there. Today, the mansion is owned by the State of Illinois and is closed to visitors.

Source: "A piece of history fading out," *Times-Leader* (McLeansboro) 9 September 1996; Scott, Beth and Michael Norman. *Haunted Heartland: True Ghost Stories from the American Midwest*. New York: Barnes & Noble Books, 1985, 1992.

The Hickory Hill Plantation is located at the end of Hickory Hill Lane, off Walnut Lane, Just south of Route 13 and west of Route 1. The mansion is not currently open to the public.

Hamilton County

Population: 8,621
County Seat: McLeansboro
Total Area: 436 square miles
Per capita income: $16,262
Year Established: 1821

McLeansboro

Lakey's Creek

The headless horseman of Lakey's Creek is quite possibly one of the oldest ghost stories in Illinois. Passed down as an oral tradition until John W. Allen put the story on paper in 1963, the mysterious man named Lakey, as well as his untimely end, has been immortalized in the folklore of Southern Illinois. Long before a concrete bridge spanned the shallow creek 1.5 miles east of McLeansboro, a frontiersman named Lakey attempted to erect his log cabin near a ford along the wagon trail to Mt. Vernon. One morning, a lone traveler stumbled upon Lakey's body. Lakey's head had been severed by his own axe, which was left at the scene.

According to legend, his murderer was never found. For decades after the murder, travelers reported being chased by a headless horseman that rode out of the woods along Lakey's Creek. "Always the rider, on a large black horse, joined travelers approaching the stream from the east, and always on the downstream side," John Allen wrote. "Each time and just before reaching the center of the creek, the mistlike figure would turn downstream and disappear." The headless horseman has been seen much less frequently in recent years.

Source: Allen, John W. *Legends & Lore of Southern Illinois*. Carbondale: Southern Illinois University, 1963, 1973; Kleen, Michael. *Paranormal Illinois*. Atglen:

Schiffer Publishing, 2010; Lewis, Chad and Terry Fisk. *The Illinois Road Guide to Haunted Locations*. Eau Claire: Unexplained Research Publishing Company, 2007.

Lakey's Creek and the concrete bridge are located along Route 14, just east of McLeansboro before 1050E.

HARDIN COUNTY

Population: 4,800
County Seat: Elizabethtown
Total Area: 182 square miles
Per capita income: $15,984
Year Established: 1839

CAVE-IN-ROCK

Cave-In-Rock State Park

Cave-in-Rock, located on the Ohio River, is one of the most notorious treasure-hunting destinations in Illinois. From the 1790s to the 1870s the area around Cave-in-Rock was plagued by river pirates, horse thieves, counterfeiters, and highwaymen. Over $1 million worth of stolen loot, gold, cash, and counterfeit bills changed hands there between 1790 and 1830 alone. In 1800, the Mason gang was rumored to have hidden a large stash of gold at Cave-in-Rock, but Samuel Mason was beheaded after he was caught on the Spanish side of the Mississippi River with $7,000 and 20 human scalps. Aside from Mason's horde, there are supposed to be dozens of stashes of gold and silver all along the cliff face. According to Troy Taylor, travelers passing on the river claim to hear moans and cries echoing from the cave.

Source: Henson, Michael Paul. *A Guide to Treasure in Illinois and Indiana*. Dona Ana: Carson Enterprises, 1982; Taylor, Troy. *Haunted Illinois: The Travel Guide to the History & Hauntings of the Prairie State*. Alton: Whitechapel Productions Press, 2004.

Cave-in-Rock State Park is located in southwestern Hardin County, along Park Ave (1435 E), just east of the Village of Cave-in-Rock.

Elizabethtown

Rose Hotel

The Rose Hotel is currently owned by the Illinois Historic Preservation Agency and operated as a bed and breakfast. Built by James McFarland *circa* 1830, with additions added in 1848 and 1866, it is the oldest active hotel in the state of Illinois. In 2009, the Little Egypt Ghost Society investigated the hotel and captured a photo of a strange reflection that appeared in the mirror of the McFarlan Suite. They compared it to photographs in an old hotel scrapbook and determined it was an image of the ghost of a former servant named Tote. Another anomalous photo appeared to show a woman in old-fashioned dress, which they believed to be a former hotel operator named Maimee Rose. The group also recorded several EVPs and heard a number of out-of-place voices.

Source: "Little Egypt Ghost Society investigates the paranormal," *Daily Register* (Harrisburg) 22 October 2009; http://www.illinoishistory.gov/hs/rose_hotel.htm.

The Rose Hotel is located at 92 Main Street in Elizabethtown, and is currently operated by Sandy Vinyard. The hotel is open during regular business hours.

Rock Creek

Rock Creek Ghost

Rock Creek was one of the many early settlements in Southern Illinois. A very well-known legend among locals there concerned a ghost that appeared in three different forms, always around the same branch of Rock Creek near a church. In the first encounter, a sheriff and his deputy were riding their horses down the road when suddenly their horses were spooked by what they described as an old-fashioned carpet-bag, which rolled toward them. The two peace officers fired their pistols at it and it vanished. The ghost's next incarnation was of a large shepherd dog that crossed the path of a group of boys who were coming home from church. One of them kicked at the dog, but his foot passed right through it as though it wasn't even there. The phantom dog continued to be seen into the early 1900s. At night, travelers often heard something following them in the brush.

Source: Neely, Charles, ed. *Tales and Songs of Southern Illinois*. Menasha: George Banta Publishing, 1938; reprint, Carbondale: Southern Illinois University Press, 1998.

Rock Creek is located at the junction of 1050E and Rock Creek Road, inside the Shawnee National Forest. The old church was located where the road crosses a branch of Rock Creek just south of that intersection.

JACKSON COUNTY

Population: 59,612
County Seat: Murphysboro
Total Area: 603 square miles
Per capita income: $15,755
Year Established: 1816

CARBONDALE

Carbondale Post Office (Former)

Now occupied by DCI Biologicals (a blood plasma center), the old Carbondale post office is a building reportedly rife with poltergeist activity. Several years ago, the figure of a woman wearing a white dress was seen in the lobby, and a "white form" appeared standing behind an employee in a photograph. Employees have seen the lobby chandelier swing back and forth, doors open by themselves, radios turn on and off at will, and at least one janitor quit because he "could not handle the intensity and frequency" of the activity. In one incident, a janitor became trapped in a closet when the door shut and locked with no apparent cause. Michelle Kell, a manager at the plasma center, has heard a phone ring in the basement even though no phones are located there.

Source: "Haunted Southern Illinois: Region Full of the Scary, Bizarre, and Freaky Phenomena," *The Southern* (Carbondale) 30 October 2004.

DCI Biologicals is located at 301 West Main Street, at the southwest corner of Main and University, in Carbondale. It is open during regular business hours.

Hundley Home

On December 12, 1928, John Charles Hundley, a former mayor of Carbondale, and his wife Luella were shot to death in their stately home. The killer was never found although their own stepson was a prime suspect in the crime. Over the years, the building has been remodeled to serve many different purposes. The room where John and Luella slept, and where they were killed, became known as "the murder room." In 2008, Dan Jones purchased the building and converted it into a bed and breakfast, despite stories of strange sounds, phantom piano music, and doors that slammed shut on their own. Having heard about the ghostly activity, Barry Klinge of the Discovery Channel's series *Ghost Lab* brought his camera crew to the home in August 2010. They walked away convinced of the validity of the haunting.

Source: "Doors Slam, Lights Flash, Disembodied Voices Speak," *The Southern* (Carbondale) 31 October 2010; "Ghost Hunting in Carbondale," *The Southern* (Carbondale) 18 August 2010; "Famous Residence Becomes B&B," *The Southern* (Carbondale) 15 May 2010.

The Hundley House Bed & Breakfast is located at 601 W. Main Street in Carbondale and is open during regular business hours. www.hundleyhouse.net

Southern Illinois University

Southern Illinois University in Carbondale was chartered in 1869 and is home to 22,550 students and faculty. In keeping with its central place in Little Egypt, the university's mascot is the Saluki, the dog of ancient Egyptian royalty. In past years, the campus experienced riotous partying around Halloween. Wheeler Hall, Faner Hall, Shryock Auditorium, and Mae Smith Residence Hall are all believed to be haunted. While a poltergeist is said to dwell in Wheeler, the ghost of a student who became lost in Faner has been seen wandering in and out of its classrooms. Shryock Auditorium was dedicated to and named after SIU's fifth president, Henry Shryock. Today, students and custodians have dubbed a safety light in the auditorium "Henry," because it appears to have a mind of its own. They have also seen a shadowy figure standing on the stage. The ghost of a broken-hearted resident assistant supposedly haunts Mae Smith Residence Hall.

Source: "If these Walls Could Talk," *Daily Egyptian* (Carbondale) 23 October 2002; "Ghost Hunting in Illinois," *Daily Egyptian* (Carbondale) 25 October 2006.

Southern Illinois University is located in the southern part of Carbondale, roughly southwest of Mill Street and Route 51. www.siu.edu.

Sunset Haven

The Jackson County Poor Farm became known as Sunset Haven during the 1940s when it was converted into a nursing home. The nursing home closed in 1957 and Southern Illinois University purchased the property to expand its agricultural program. During the 1970s, the university made an effort to locate all the unmarked graves of the dead that had been buried during Sunset Haven's years as a poor farm. The graves are supposedly located in a grove of trees behind the building. Sometime later, the name was changed again, this time to the "Vivarium Annex," where SIU used it for animal research. The building is currently abandoned, although the university occasionally stages emergency drills on the property to test its medical students. The building's final closure and decay inevitably led to stories of ghosts and other horrors, and the atmosphere inside the structure lent itself to rumors of medical experiments gone awry.

Source: Kleen, Michael. "Sunset Haven." *Legends and Lore of Illinois 2* (February 2008): 1-7; Taylor, Troy. *Haunted Illinois: The Travel Guide to the History & Hauntings of the Prairie State.* Alton: Whitechapel Productions Press, 2004.

Sunset Haven is located along Autumn Point Drive, off Chautauqua Road, west of the campus of Southern Illinois University. This is private property.

GRAND TOWER

Devil's Bake-Oven

A cave along the banks of the Mississippi River called the Devil's Bake-Oven is home to one of the area's oldest and most famous legends. According to this legend, a young woman named Esmerelda fell in love with a riverboat captain, but her father disapproved of the courtship. One day, word came that her lover had been killed in a boiler explosion. Grief stricken, Esmerelda leapt to her death into the rushing waters of the Mississippi.

To this day, visitors have reported seeing a white specter in and around Devil's Bake-Oven. Shrieks, sobbing, and moans have often accompanied this apparition. Local historian Charles Burdick believes the legend may be based in fact. Evidence, such as an old foundation hidden near the river and a few surviving photographs of a white manor house, helps lend credence to the story.

Source: "Esmerelda Haunts Devil's Bake-Oven in Grand Tower," *The Southern* (Carbondale) 28 October 2005; Burdick, Charles. *History of Grand Tower, Illinois: 1800-2000.* By the author, 2000; Taylor, Troy. *Haunted Illinois: The Travel Guide to the History & Hauntings of the Prairie State.* Alton: Whitechapel Productions Press, 2004.

The Devil's Bake-Oven is located just northwest of the town of Grand Tower, off Park Road (20th St.) along the Mississippi River.

MURPHYSBORO

Murphysboro Mud Monster

The wilds of Southern Illinois have long produced tales of strange creatures, and the Mud Monster—or "Big Muddy"—is no exception. This hairy, smelly biped was seen several times in the summer of 1973 lurking near Murphysboro along the banks of the Big Muddy River. Like Peoria's Cole

Haunting Illinois: Little Egypt | 171

Hollow Road Monster, the Murphysboro creature was described as being seven feet tall and covered in matted, white fur. Police officers found several tracks at the scene of the first sighting and even heard its "inhuman" cry. The next night, a young boy and two of his neighbors saw the creature when it wandered through their backyards. After a few weeks of intense scrutiny, the Murphysboro Mud Monster disappeared as mysteriously as it arrived.

Source: Taylor, Troy. *Weird Illinois: Your Travel Guide to Illinois' Local Legends and Best Kept Secrets.* New York: Sterling Publishing, 2005.

Murphysboro is located north of the Big Muddy River, at the juncture of Route 13, 127, and 149, a few miles northwest of Carbondale.

JEFFERSON COUNTY

Population: 40,045
County Seat: Mount Vernon
Total Area: 584 square miles
Per capita income: $16,644
Year Established: 1819

MOUNT VERNON

"Black Annie"

Between the late 1860s and the early 1930s, Mount Vernon was plagued by the appearance of a female spirit known variously as "Black Annie," "Lady of Sorrow," or "Cyclone Annie." According to Michael Norman, sightings of Annie began when the citizens of Mount Vernon ran off a witch who was threatening their cattle. They thought they were rid of her, until February 9, 1888, when a tornado touched down in Mount Vernon and destroyed a half-mile-wide swath of homes and businesses, killing 37 and injuring as many as 800 people. After the disaster, several eyewitnesses reported seeing a woman dressed in black—wailing and screaming—wandering among the debris. In 1918, residents of Mount Vernon were terrified by the appearance of a woman dressed in black who chased pedestrians, in much the same manner of the "lady in black" encountered in McDonough County.

172 | Michael Kleen

Finally, "Black Annie" was blamed for a series of strange attacks in 1936 involving sleeping powder thrown through open windows. She has not been seen since, but parents sometimes use "Black Annie" to scare their children into behaving properly.

Source: "The Mt. Vernon Disaster," *Daily Republican* (Decatur) 23 February 1888; Norman, Michael. *Haunted Homeland: A Definitive Collection of North American Ghost Stories.* New York: Tor Books, 2006.

Mount Vernon is located at the juncture of Route 15 and Route 37, northeast of Interstate 64 and 57.

LAWRENCE COUNTY

Population: 15,452
County Seat: Lawrenceville
Total Area: 374 square miles
Per capita income: $17,070
Year Established: 1821

LAWRENCEVILLE

Lawrenceville High School

On May 23, 1845, Elizabeth Reed was executed for the crime of poisoning her husband with arsenic. Between 10,000 and 20,000 spectators witnessed her death, and Elizabeth became notorious as the only woman to ever have been hanged in the State of Illinois. Years later, her place of execution was leveled and replaced by the Lawrenceville High School football field. The high school was built in 1915. In 1952, a young woman took the job of librarian at the school, and shortly after, her ex-fiancé, an alcoholic with a troubled past, gunned her down in the hallway. Students quickly began to believe that the young woman's ghost haunted the school. In 1975, a group of football players encountered something strange in the darkened building after a game. One of the boys saw a woman standing behind him when he left the locker room to get a drink. He ran, but when he turned around, the woman had disappeared. The other football players proceeded to search the school and witnessed what they described as a "grayish tan" figure at various places in the building.

Source: Taylor, Troy. *Haunted Illinois: The Travel Guide to the History & Hauntings of the Prairie State.* Alton: Whitechapel Productions Press, 2004.

Lawrenceville High School is located at 503 8th Street.
The building is not open to the general public.

Marion County

Population: 41,691
County Seat: Salem
Total Area: 576 square miles
Per capita income: $17,235
Year Established: 1823

Centralia

Elmwood Cemetery

Originally called Centralia Cemetery, this graveyard was in use in the 1860s but not officially established until 1877. Its name was changed to Elmwood Cemetery in 1921. A popular local legend maintains that the sweet strains of a violin can be heard emanating from the cemetery at night. The origin of these ethereal notes is said to be none other than the statue of "Violin Annie." Deep inside Elmwood sits a large monument shaped like a tabernacle or an ancient Greek temple with only four columns. At the top of the monument stands a nearly life-sized statue of a young girl with flowing locks of hair. In her hands she holds a violin. The statue depicts Harriet Annie, the daughter of Dr. Winfield and Eoline Marshall. Annie died of diphtheria in 1890, a few weeks after her eleventh birthday. Some locals also believe that Annie's statue glows on Halloween night.

Source: Kleen, Michael. "Elmwood Cemetery." *Legends and Lore of Illinois* 3 (April 2009): 1-8; Lewis, Chad and Terry Fisk. *The Illinois Road Guide to Haunted Locations*. Eau Claire: Unexplained Research Publishing Company, 2007.

Elmwood Cemetery is located off Sycamore and Gragg streets, just north of Centralia, at the border of Central City. The cemetery closes at dusk.

ROMINE TOWNSHIP

James Gregory Stash

Between 1880 and 1925, a man named James Gregory operated the only dry goods store south of Hickory Hill Church. Over the years, he became wealthy supplying local farmers with all their equipment, feed, and other supplies, but like many rural residents in the late nineteenth century, James did not trust banks. He apparently did not trust his own wife either, because she had no knowledge of where he hid his money. Neighbors, however, sometimes observed that he would duck out to a pasture behind his home whenever he needed to stock up on additional inventory. In 1925, he suffered a stroke and died. His wife searched for her inheritance in vain, and there are believed to be several thousand dollars still hidden somewhere on his former property.

Source: Henson, Michael Paul. *A Guide to Treasure in Illinois and Indiana*. Dona Ana: Carson Enterprises, 1982.

The James Gregory farm was located just south of Hickory Hill Church. Hickory Hill Cemetery is still located off a narrow road at the junction of 2125 E and County Highway 30.

Wamac

1947 Centralia Mine Disaster

On March 25, 1947, Centralia Coal Company Mine No. 5 exploded with 142 people inside. Sixty-five miners died instantly due to severe burns, while forty-five were killed by afterdamp, a toxic mixture of carbon dioxide, carbon monoxide, and nitrogen released by the explosion. Miraculously, eight miners survived trapped under the surface and were rescued, but one succumbed to his injuries. Woody Guthrie's song "The Dying Miner" is about the disaster, and the site is now marked by a memorial plaque.

Source: Hartley, Robert E. and David Kenney, *Death Underground: The Centralia and West Frankfort Mine Disasters*. Carbondale: Southern Illinois University Press, 2006.

The site of the Centralia Mine Disaster is now the location of Wamac City Park, along Wabash Avenue. Wamac sits on the county line, just south of Centralia.

Massac County

Population: 15,161
County Seat: Metropolis
Total Area: 242 square miles
Per capita income: $16,334
Year Established: 1843

Brookport

Kincaid Mounds

The Kincaid Mounds sit astride the Ohio River, just across the border from Kentucky. In addition to the mound complex at Cahokia, Kincaid Mounds Historic Site was formerly a powerful city center in the Mississippian culture from 1050 to 1400 AD, although there is evidence of even older human habitation at the site. The central mounds are as tall as 30 feet with one being 500 feet long. Like Cahokia, the people who lived at Kincaid Mounds vanished long before French explorers arrived, but no American Indian tribes were known to inhabit the area.

Source: Cole, Fay-Cooper, et al. *Kincaid: A Prehistoric Illinois Metropolis*. Chicago: University of Chicago Press, 1951; http://www.south ernmostillinoishistory.net/kincaid2.htm.

Kincaid Mounds State Historic Site is located along Kincaid Road, off New Cut Road, about seven miles southeast of Brookport. The park closes at dusk. www.kincaidmounds.com.

Perry County

Population: 23,094
County Seat: Pinckneyville
Total Area: 447 square miles
Per capita income: $15,935
Year Established: 1827

Pyramid State Park

Stump Pond Serpent

Midwesterners love to hunt and fish, and this is especially true in the forests and lakes of Southern Illinois. Between 1879 and 1968, nearly a 90-year period, fishermen in Perry County spun yarns about a serpent that dwelled in the murky waters of Stump Pond. The creature was described as having a thick, green body with black fins. It was large enough to rock boats. Some fishermen encountered it more than once and speculated that there must be a breeding population. Unfortunately, no one ever caught the alleged serpent, and when the lake was partially drained in 1968, locals discovered catfish that weighed over 30 pounds. It is possible that the "Stump Pond Serpent" was a giant catfish, which have been known to grow to the size of a small child. In 2005 Tim Pruitt of Alton caught a 124-pound blue catfish in the Mississippi River. Today, Stump Pond is a part of Pyramid State Recreation Area, which consists of land formerly owned by a coal strip-mining company.

Source: Taylor, Troy. *Weird Illinois: Your Travel Guide to Illinois' Local Legends and Best Kept Secrets.* New York: Sterling Publishing, 2005.

Stump Pond is located in the Pyramid State Recreation Area, just south of Galum Church Road and north of the Wesseln Cut. The park closes at dusk.

POPE COUNTY

Population: 4,413
County Seat: Golconda
Total Area: 375 square miles
Per capita income: $16,440
Year Established: 1816

THE GOOSENECK

Haunted Cabin

Titled "The Miser's Gold" in Charles Neely's collection of folktales from Southern Illinois, this story is nearly identical to the one told about the cabin near Kingston in Adams County. This story takes place "in the early days of Pope County" (c.1820s) and concerns a family from Kentucky who took shelter in a cabin near the Ohio River. The cabin had been owned by a wealthy elderly hermit who was murdered by thieves, and neighbors believed it was so haunted that no one could live there. The wife was a devout Christian, however, and was unafraid of the ghost. When the ghost appeared, she asked him what he wanted, and he told her where to dig to find a pot of gold in the cellar. Sure enough, when her husband returned, the two dug where the ghost had indicated and discovered a small fortune.

Source: Neely, Charles, ed. *Tales and Songs of Southern Illinois.* Menasha: George Banta Publishing, 1938; reprint, Carbondale: Southern Illinois University Press, 1998.

This haunted cabin was located in the "Gooseneck" of Pope County, which was the narrow strip of land at the southern half of the county. Much of this land is now part of the Shawnee National Forest.

PULASKI COUNTY

Population: 7,348
County Seat: Mound City
Total Area: 203 square miles
Per capita income: $13,325
Year Established: 1843

MOUND CITY

Mound City National Cemetery

Established in 1862 during the Civil War, Mound City National Cemetery is a military cemetery that contains the bodies of 2,700 unknown Union soldiers. Army nurses, Confederate soldiers, spies, and even the colorful Russian officer General John B. Turchin (Ivan Vasilyevich Turchaninov), are also buried here. The cemetery is allegedly haunted by Turchin's wife, Nadine (Nadezhda), who has been seen wandering the grounds in a white dress. General Turchin served in the Union army during the Civil War and afterward came to live in Washington County. After his death at an institution in Anna, his wife mourned at his graveside until her own life ended a few years later and she was interred next to him. Visitors to the cemetery have also reported seeing lights in an old abandoned caretaker's house.

Source: http://en.wikipedia.org/wiki/John_B._Turchin; Taylor, Troy. *Haunted Illinois: The Travel Guide to the History & Hauntings of the Prairie State*. Alton: Whitechapel Productions Press, 2004.

Mound City National Cemetery is located at the juncture of Route 37 (Walnut Street) and Old US Highway 51, just northwest of Mound City and the Ohio River. The cemetery closes at dusk.

Haunting Illinois: Little Egypt | 179

Pulaski County Courthouse

Ghostly encounters at the Pulaski County Courthouse go back at least three decades, and local resident Cleo King has been there in one capacity or another for most of them. The courthouse was built in 1911, and its basement was formerly home to the county jail, before it was recently remodeled. The earliest encounter King recalled was when a fellow student at Lovejoy School, located across the street from the courthouse, saw a man hanging from the tree in the courthouse lawn. No one had been hanged in Pulaski County for many, many years. According to King, the courthouse is haunted by four ghosts. One, the man seen swinging from the tree, was the last man hanged in the county. He usually haunts the former jail in the basement. The other three ghosts are that of an elderly black woman, an anonymous lady called the "Taffeta Woman" who is believed to have died in an accident, and the ghost of a former attorney who makes his presence known with thick cigar smoke.

Source: "Pulaski's Haunted Court House: Four Ghosts Roam this 1911 Building, Still Waiting for Justice," *The Southern* (Carbondale) 30 October 2004.

The Pulaski County Courthouse is located at 500 Illinois Avenue in Mound City. www.pulaskicountyil.net

Randolph County

Population: 33,893
County Seat: Chester
Total Area: 597 square miles
Per capita income: $17,696
Year Established: 1795

Chester

Colonel Clark's Lost Silver

George Rogers Clark is a celebrated name in Illinois history. In 1778, as the Revolutionary War raged out east, Clark asked Patrick Henry (then Governor of Virginia) for permission to lead a secret expedition to capture British posts in the Illinois country, which included Kaskaskia, Cahokia, and

Vincennes. Patrick Henry commissioned Clark as a lieutenant colonel in the Virginia militia and authorized him to raise troops. Before his 175-man army left, the Virginia governor gave him several thousand pounds silver sterling to pay for the expedition. As Clark's army was preparing to attack Fort Kaskaskia on July 4, they buried 1,200 pounds sterling west of present day Steeleville, near the Mississippi River, in case things went badly. He was victorious in battle, but unfortunately, the Mississippi flooded and obscured the location of the coins. This money has never been recovered.

Source: Henson, Michael Paul. *A Guide to Treasure in Illinois and Indiana*. Dona Ana: Carson Enterprises, 1982.

The exact location of Colonel Clark's lost silver is, of course, unknown. However, the only town west of Steeleville and south of Fort Kaskaskia is Chester. Kaskaskia Street runs along the river there.

RICHLAND COUNTY

Population: 16,149
County Seat: Olney
Total Area: 362 square miles
Per capita income: $16,847
Year Established: 1841

CLAREMONT

Mt. Pleasant Cemetery

Mt. Pleasant Church and Cemetery are relatively new additions to local lore, having developed their legends within the past few decades. The church, which closed in 1990, is said to be home to a variety of phenomenon. Visitors have reported hearing choirs and footsteps and have witnessed lights emanating from the cracks in the door. There are also rumors of phantom funerals at

Haunting Illinois: Little Egypt

the cemetery. As of yet, very little of the information regarding this location has been confirmed.

Source: Kleen, Michael. "Mt. Pleasant Cemetery." *Legends and Lore of Illinois* 1 (November 2007): 1-6.

> *Mt. Pleasant Church and Cemetery is located on a hill overlooking the intersection of 800N (Mt. Pleasant Lane) and 1700E, about two miles south of Claremont. The cemetery closes at dusk.*

DECKER TOWNSHIP

Burrows Cave

In the early 1980s, a man named Russell Burrows claimed to stumble upon a hidden cave somewhere near Olney. Even more incredible were the artifacts he said were hidden there. He found human remains, metal weapons, and an ancient language carved into gold tablets. Stranger still, the language was Middle Eastern and European in origin, and not from any known American Indian culture. According to Burrows, "The artifacts include ax heads of marble and other stone material, an ax head of what appears to be bronze, a short sword of what appears to be bronze, and other artifacts which might be considered personal weapons." The find excited archeologists who believed that ancient cultures had interacted across continents. Unfortunately, Burrows refused to reveal the location of the cave to mainstream scientists, and the artifacts that allegedly came from the site were all shown to be frauds. After decades of debate, the Burrows Cave is now widely believed to have been an elaborate hoax.

Source: Burrows, Russell and Fred Rydholm. *The Mystery Cave of Many Faces: First in a Series on the Saga of Burrows' Cave.* Superior Heartland, 1992; http://www.bibliotecapleyades.net/sociopolitica/ esp_sociopol_underground12.htm; http://www.showcaves.com/english/usa /caves/Burr ows.html.

> *Burrows cave is allegedly located somewhere in the southwest corner of Richland County near the Little Wabash River.*

Union County

Population: 18,293
County Seat: Jonesboro
Total Area: 422 square miles
Per capita income: $16,450
Year Established: 1818

Anna

Choate Mental Health Center

The Choate Mental Health Center was originally called the Southern Hospital for the Insane. It was built in 1869 and opened in 1875. A fire destroyed a wing of the main building (called Kirkbride after the doctor who designed it) in 1881, and another fire destroyed a large section of the hospital in 1895. Tunnels connect the various buildings. The hospital has been rumored to be haunted for many years. Visitors and passersby have witnessed apparitions, figures, and faces in the windows. One popular story recounts that a "devil dog" attacked a patient in his room at night. When orderlies turned on the lights, they found scratches all over his body. The tunnels below the buildings are also supposed to be very haunted, and at least one person who went down there felt like he was touched by something unseen.

Source: Committee on State Charitable Institutions. *Brief History of the Charitable Institutions of the State of Illinois.* Chicago: John Morris, 1893; http://www.carolyar.com/Illinois/Misc/Anna.htm; http://theshadowlands.net/places/illinois.htm.

The Choate Mental Health Center is located at 1000 N. Main Street, just north of Anna. The hospital is not open to the general public.

JONESBORO

Dug Hill Road

The first story concerning Dug Hill is a classic haunting rooted in the past. In 1863, Union army deserters ambushed and killed a provost marshal named Welch along Dug Hill Road. There are two versions of the story, one involving three deserters, the other involving a dozen or so. In the second version, Welch's own friend betrayed him and led him into the ambush. Since then, his ghost has been seen along the road. Another legend concerns a man named Bill Smith, who reportedly witnessed a spectral wagon pass over his head. The wagon was typical ghoulish fare—pulled by a pair of black horses.

A third story pertaining to the Dug Hill area concerns a creature known as "the boger." The boger, or the boger-man, was something cooked up by parents who want to scare their children. Two men have reportedly seen this boger along Dug Hill Road in the past. The creature appears as a nine- to eleven-foot-tall man who wears black pants, a white shirt, and a long scarf. No one has yet come forward to explain where this creature found someone to tailor his gigantic clothes.

Source: Kleen, Michael. *Paranormal Illinois*. Atglen: Schiffer Publishing, 2010; Neely, Charles, ed. *Tales and Songs of Southern Illinois*. Menasha: George Banta Publishing, 1938; reprint, Carbondale: Southern Illinois University Press, 1998.

The old Dug Hill Road is today known as Route 146 and runs through the Shawnee National Forest west of Anna.

184 | *Michael Kleen*

Washington County

Population: 15,148
County Seat: Nashville
Total Area: 564 square miles
Per capita income: $19,108
Year Established: 1818

Okawville

Original Springs Hotel

During the late 1800s, Okawville was widely known for its mineral springs, which were believed to have an invigorating effect on health. After the particular quality of the springs was discovered in 1867, a local businessman and a farmer established the first bathhouse and spa at the location. That burnt down in 1891, and the current building, which became the Original Springs Hotel, opened in the spring of 1893. The hotel is still in operation today, although it has had many owners. One previous owner, Tom Rogers, died in an upstairs room in 1962.

Guests at the hotel have reported seeing a mysterious woman wearing a white dress in the fashion of the early 1900s sitting on the second floor balcony. Her face is always hidden beneath her hat. One guest reported seeing her standing near his bed, and another saw her staring out the window of a locked storage room in the men's bathhouse. Ethereal music has also been heard in the laundry room.

Source: "A Haunted Hunt," *The Southern* (Carbondale) 26 October 2007; Taylor, Troy. *Haunted Illinois: The Travel Guide to the History & Hauntings of the Prairie State*. Alton: Whitechapel Productions Press, 2004.

The Original Springs Motel is located at 506 N. Hanover Street in Okawville and is open during regular business hours. www.theoriginalspringshotel.com

White County

Population: 15,371
County Seat: Carmi
Total Area: 502 square miles
Per capita income: $16,412
Year Established: 1815

Enfield

Enfield Horror

For some unknown reason, the 1970s saw a renaissance in fortean-creature sightings in Illinois, and the Enfield Horror was truly the strangest of them all. In the spring of 1973, a bizarre and deformed creature terrorized the community of Enfield. Eyewitnesses described it as short, with small arms like a T-Rex, broad, pink eyes, grayish skin, and three legs. On April 25, 1973, it attacked a young boy who was playing in his yard then attempted to break into a nearby home. The homeowner shot the monster, and it fled. Rick Rainbow, an Indiana resident and news director for WWKI Radio, managed to record its cries. One common element in all the sightings was that they occurred near railroad tracks. By June, sightings stopped, and this creature—like the others—vanished without a trace.

Source: Taylor, Troy. *Weird Illinois: Your Travel Guide to Illinois' Local Legends and Best Kept Secrets*. New York: Sterling Publishing, 2005.

Enfield is located along Route 45, just north of Route 14, about 10 miles west of McLeansboro.

WILLIAMSON COUNTY

Population: 61,296
County Seat: Marion
Total Area: 444 square miles
Per capita income: $17,779
Year Established: 1839

HERRIN

The Herrin Massacre

On June 22, 1922, members of the United Mine Workers of America surrounded and besieged a strip mine located between Herrin and Marion after its owner, W. J. Lester, disregarded a deal with the union and brought in strikebreakers and private guards to ship out the coal he had mined under their agreement. With tensions at a boiling point, local authorities did nothing to stop the mob from looting guns from the Herrin hardware store or from attacking the mine. After the strikebreakers surrendered, the union men marched their prisoners west to a wooded area and shot them. Those who escaped were either gunned down in Herrin Cemetery or in the nearby woods. The throats of the wounded men in the cemetery were cut with a pocket knife. In all, 19 strikebreakers along with 2 union men who had been shot during the siege were killed. Members of the union were acquitted on all charges, despite widespread outrage and calls for justice.

Source: Angle, Paul M. *Bloody Williamson: A Chapter in American Lawlessness.* Urbana: University of Illinois Press, 1952, 1992.

The Herrin Massacre occurred in Powerhouse Woods, Harrison Woods, and the old section of Herrin Cemetery. The cemetery is located east of Herrin along Stotlar Street. The woods were located directly southwest of the cemetery, and north of Crenshaw Road.

FURTHER READING

Adams, Len. *Phantoms in the Looking Glass: History and Hauntings of the Illinois Prairie.* Decatur: Whitechapel Press, 2008.

Allen, John W. *Legends & Lore of Southern Illinois.* Carbondale: Southern Illinois University, 1963, 1973.

Allen-Kline, Margaret. "'She Protects Her Girls': The Legend of Mary Hawkins at Pemberton Hall." M.A. thesis, Eastern Illinois University, 1998.

Bielski, Ursula. *Chicago Haunts: Ghostlore of the Windy City.* Chicago: Lake Claremont Press, 1998.

_____. *More Chicago Haunts: Scenes from Myth and Memory.* Chicago: Lake Claremont Press, 2000.

_____. *Chicago Haunts 3: Locked Up Stories from an October City.* Holt: Thunder Bay Press, 2009.

Brandon, Trent. *The Book of Ghosts.* Galloway: Zerotime Publishing, 2003.

Brooks, Rachel. *Chicago Ghosts.* Atglen: Schiffer Publishing, 2008.

_____. *Ghosts of Springfield and Southern Illinois.* Atglen: Schiffer Publishing, 2009.

Brunvand, Jan Harold. *The Mexican pet: More "New" Urban Legends and Some Old Favorites.* New York: W.W. Norton & Company, 1986.

_____. *The Vanishing Hitchhiker: American Urban Legends and Their Meanings.* New York: W.W. Norton & Company, 1981.

Burrows, Russell and Fred Rydholm. *The Mystery Cave of Many Faces: First in a Series on the Saga of Burrows' Cave.* Superior Heartland, 1992.

Christensen, Jo-Anne. *Ghost Stories of Illinois.* Edmonton: Lone Pine, 2000.

Clark, Jerome. *Unnatural Phenomena: A Guide to the Bizarre Wonders of North America* (Santa Barbara: ABC-CLIO, 2005).

Cole, Fay-Cooper, et al. *Kincaid: A Prehistoric Illinois Metropolis.* Chicago: University of Chicago Press, 1951.

Committee on State Charitable Institutions. *Brief History of the Charitable Institutions of the State of Illinois.* Chicago: John Morris, 1893.

Corliss, William R. *Handbook of Unusual Natural Phenomena: Eyewitness Accounts of Nature's Greatest Mysteries.* New York: Arlington House, 1986.

Carlson, Bruce. *Ghosts of Rock Island County, Illinois.* Fort Madison: Quixote Press, 1987.

Crowe, Richard T. *Chicago's Street Guide to the Supernatural.* Oak Park: Carolando Press, 2000, 2001.

Emerson, Thomas and Barry Lewis. *Cahokia and the Hinterlands: Middle Mississipian Cultures of the Midwest.* Urbana, Illinois: University of Illinois Press, 1991.

Frantz, Kevin J. *Naperville, Chicago's Haunted Heighbor, Vol. 1.* Naperville: Unrested Dead Publishing, 2008.

Gorman, William. *Ghost Whispers: Tales from Haunted Midway.* Rockford: Helm Publishing, 2005.

Graczyk, Jim and Donna Boonstra. *Field Guide to Illinois Hauntings.* Alton: Whitechapel Productions Press, 2001.

Guiley, Rosemary Ellen. *The Complete Vampire Companion.* New York: Macmillan, 1994.

Hauck, Dennis William. *Haunted Places: The National Directory: Ghostly Abodes, Sacred Sites, UFO Landings, and Other Supernatural Locations.* New York: Penguin Books, 1994, 1996.

Heise, Kenan. *Resurrection Mary: a Ghost Story.* Evanston: Chicago Historical Bookworks, 1990.

Henson, Michael Paul. *A Guide to Treasure in Illinois and Indiana.* Dona Ana: Carson Enterprises, 1982.

Hucke, Matt and Ursula Bielski. *Graveyards of Chicago: The People, History, Art, and Lore of Cook County Cemeteries.* Chicago: Lake Claremont Press, 1999.

Hyatt, Harry Middleton. *Folk-lore from Adams County, Illinois.* Alma Egan Hyatt Foundation, 1935.

Kachuba, John B. *Ghosthunting Illinois.* Cincinnati: Clerisy Press, 2005.

Kaczmarek, Dale. *Illuminating the Darkness: The Mystery of Spook Lights.* Oak Lawn: Ghost Research Society Press, 2003.

_____. *Windy City Ghosts: An Essential Guide to the Haunted History of Chicago.* Oak Lawn: Ghost Research Society Press, 2000, 2005.

_____. *Windy City Ghosts II: More tales from America's most haunted city.* Oak Lawn: Ghost Research Society Press, 2005.

Kleen, Michael. *Legends and Lore of Illinois.* Vol. 1-4. Charleston/Rockford: Black Oak Press, Illinois, 2007-2010.

_____. *Legends and Lore of Illinois: Case Files.* Vol. 1. Rockford: Black Oak Press, Illinois, 2009.

_____. *Legends and Lore of Coles County, Illinois.* Issues 1-9. Charleston: Black Oak Press, Illinois, 2006.

_____. *Paranormal Illinois.* Atglen: Schiffer Publishing, 2010.

_____. *The Legend of Pemberton Hall.* Charleston: Black Oak Press, Illinois, 2008.

Ladley, Diane A. *Haunted Aurora.* Charleston: The History Press, 2010.

_____. *Haunted Naperville.* Chicago: Acadia Publishing, 2009.

Lewis, Chad and Terry Fisk. *The Illinois Road Guide to Haunted Locations.* Eau Claire: Unexplained Research Publishing, 2007.

Lisman, Gary. *Bittersweet Memories: a History of the Peoria State Hospital.* Victoria: Trafford Publishing, 2005.

Markus, Scott. *Voices from the Chicago Grave: They're Calling. Will You Answer?* Holt: Thunder Bay Press, 2008.

McCarthy, Stephanie E. *Haunted Peoria.* Chicago: Arcadia Publishing, 2009.

McCarty, Michael and Connie Corcoran Wilson. *Ghostly Tales of Route 66: from Chicago to Oklahoma.* Wever: Quixote Press, 2008.

Neely, Charles, ed. *Tales and Songs of Southern Illinois.* Menasha: George Banta Publishing, 1938; reprint, Carbondale: Southern Illinois University Press, 1998.

Norman, Michael. *Haunted Homeland: A Definitive Collection of North American Ghost Stories.* New York: Tor Books, 2006.

Nowlan, James D. "From Lincoln to Forgottonia." *Illinois Issues* 24 (September 1998): 27-30.

Perry, Charles William. "Angeline Vernon Milner." *The Alumni Quarterly* 13 (May 1924): 2-10.

Rowe, Bill. "Was Byron's Barefoot Phantom Merely a Masquerade?" *Rockford Magazine* 11 (Fall 1996): 24-25.

Schwartz, Alvin. *Scary Stories Treasury: Three Books to Chill Your Bones.* Vol. 2, More Scary Stories to Tell in the Dark. New York: Harper Collins, 1984.

Scott, Beth and Michael Norman. *Haunted Heartland: True Ghost Stories from the American Midwest.* New York: Barnes & Noble Books, 1985, 1992.

Stanton, Carl L. *They Called it Treason: an Account of Renegades, Copperheads, Guerrillas, Bushwhackers and Outlaw Gangs that Terrorized Illinois During the Civil War.* Bunker Hill: by the author, 2002.

Stout, Steve. *The Starved Rock Murders.* Utica: Utica House Publishing, 1982.

Taylor, Troy. *Beyond the Grave: The History of America's Most Haunted Graveyards.* Alton: Whitechapel Productions Press, 2001.

_____. *Flickering Images: The History & Hauntings of the Avon Theater.* Alton: Whitechapel Productions Press, 2001.

_____. *Ghosts of Millikin: The History & Hauntings of Millikin University.* Alton: Whitechapel Productions Press, 2001.

_____. *Haunted Alton: History & Hauntings of the Riverbend Region.* Alton: Whitechapel Productions Press, 1999.

_____. *Haunted Decatur Revisited: Ghostly Tales from the Haunted Heartland of Illinois.* Alton: Whitechapel Productions Press, 2000.

_____. *Haunted Illinois: Travel Guide to the History and Hauntings of the Prairie State.* Alton: Whitechapel Productions Press, 2004.

_____. *Weird Illinois: Your Travel Guide to Illinois' Local Legends and Best Kept Secrets.* New York: Sterling Publishing, 2005.

_____. *Where the Dead Walk: History & Hauntings of Greenwood Cemetery.* Alton: Whitechapel Productions Press, 2002.

Thuma, Cynthia and Catherine Lower. *Creepy Colleges and Haunted Universities.* Atglen: Schiffer Publishing, 2003.

Watson, Daryl. *Ghosts of Galena.* Galena: Galena/Jo Daviess County Historical Society, 1995. Reprint, Dubuque: Welu Printing Company, 2005.

Zeller, George Anthony. *Befriending the Bereft.* Peoria State Hospital: by the author, 1938.

APPENDIX A

ARTICLES AND NEWS REPORTS FEATURING THE AUTHOR

"Western's Ghost Writer," *Western Illinois Magazine* 1 (Fall 2010): 16-17.

"'Tales of Coles County' features spooky stories," *Daily Eastern News* (Charleston) 28 October 2010.

"Sunset Haven: the Asylum That Never Was," *Volunteer News* (Carterville) 7 October 2010.

"Sunset Haven: A Rich, Mysterious History," *Daily Egyptian* (Carbondale) 11 August 2010.

"Local Haunts — Author explores ghostly tales across Illinois," *Times* (Streator) 24 June 2010.

"Three Coles County legends are detailed in book," *Journal Gazette* (Mattoon) 27 April 2010.

"Things that go Bump in the Night," *McDonough County Choice* (Macomb) 9 March 2010.

"Grad student masters the macabre," *Western Courier* (Macomb) 15 February 2010.

"Haunted Rockford Special Report 2," WTVO Channel 17 (Rockford) 30 October 2009.

"Charleston is Haunted," *Daily Eastern News* (Charleston) 30 October 2009.

"The Science of Spirit-Sleuthing Part III: Local Lore," *Rock River Times* (Rockford) October 28, 2009.

"Publication highlights Moon Point Cemetery," *Times* (Streator) 1 June 2009.

"Real Folklore," *Daily News* (Effingham) 21 February 2009.

"Pemberton's legend, Mary," *Daily Eastern News* (Charleston) 31 October 2008.

"Ashmore Haunted House Gets National Attention," WCIA Channel 3 (Champaign) 2 July 2008.

"Twisted tales," *Times-Courier* (Charleston) 23 October 2007.

"Ghost Club hunts for haunts," *Daily Eastern News* (Charleston) 8 October 2007.

"Student author gets creative with Coles history," *Daily Eastern News* (Charleston) 28 October 2005.

"Strange Occurrences," *Daily Eastern News* (Charleston) 28 October 2005.

"Haunting Club," *Daily Eastern News* (Charleston) 29 October 2004.

APPENDIX B

ILLINOIS PARANORMAL RESEARCH GROUPS
(Arranged by year of founding)

1977

Ghost Trackers Club/Ghost Research Society
www.ghostresearch.org

1992

Midwest Paranormal Society
www.hauntedmidwest.org

1996

American Ghost Society
www.prairieghosts.com/ags.html

Central Illinois Investigative Team
www.myspace.com/cipiteam

1998

Haunted Chicagoland/Joliet Paranormal Society
www.jolietparanormal.com

The Fallen
www.trueillinoishaunts.com/the-fallen/

1999

Illinois Paranormal Society
www.illinoisparanormalsociety.webs.com

2001

Crawford County Ghost Hunters
www.crawfordcountyghosthunters.com

2002

Christian County Ghost Hunters Society
www.parastudies.ning.com

2004

(SciFi Channel's *Ghost Hunters* premiered on October 6, 2004)

Southern Illinois Ghost Hunting Team
www.sight1.tk

Will County Ghost Hunters Society
www.aghostpage.com

2005

Northern Illinois Paranormal Investigation Society
www.nipis.org

Shelby Paranormal Research Society
www.myspace.com/shelbyparanormalsociety

2006

Chicago Paranormal Research Society
www.chicagoparanormal.org

Confidential Paranormal Investigators
www.cpiteam.net

Illinois Ghost Hunters
www.illinoisghosthunters.com

Paranormal Anomaly Search Team
www.pastinvestigators.com

Paranormal Moms Society
www.paranormalmomssociety.com

Springfield Paranormal Research Group
www.springfieldparanormal.info

Haunting the Illinois | 195

2007

DuPage Paranormal Society
www.dupageparanormal.com

Elgin Paranormal Investigators
www.elginparanormalinvestigators.com

Ghost and Paranormal Society
www.theghostandparanormalsociety.yolasite.com

Illinois Paranormal Society
www.myspace.com/illinoisparanormalsc

Insight Dimension Paranormal Research Group
www.nitey-niteghosttours.com

Little Egypt Ghost Society

New Age Paranormal
www.newageparanormal.com

Southern Illinois Ghost Hunting Society
www.sigh-il.tripod.com

2008

Central Illinois Paranormal Investigators
www.cipi.us.com

Dekalb County Paranormal Society

Dupage Researchers and Investigators of the Paranormal
www.driparanormal.com

Ghost Unit Analysis Research Detection
www.freewebs.com/ghost_unit_analysis_research_detection

Paranormal Research of Illinois
www.paranormal-research-of-illinois.com

Prairieland Paranormal Society
www.myspace.com/prairielandparanormal

Research Investigators of Paranormal

River Town Paranormal Society
www.RiverTownParanormalSociety.net

Rockford Interdisciplinary Para-investigations
www.facebook.com/RockfordRIP

Windy City Paranormal
www.windycityparanormal.com

2009

Forest City Paranormal Society
www.forest-city-paranormal-society.com

Rural Illinois Paranormal Society

Wabash Area Paranormal Society
www.wabashghosthunters.com

2010

River to River Paranormal Group

INDEX

A

Albino Tracks, The 159
Ashmore Estates 139

B

Bailey, Harvey John 48
Bar/Pub
   Brewhouse (Former) 130
   Bucktown Pub 54
   Cigars & Stripes 53
   Dormitory, The 103
   Ethyl's Party 55
   Ole St. Andrews Inn 56
   Parkway Inn 103
   Sober Duck 130
   Spirits Lounge 152
   Tito's on the Edge 55
   Tonic Room 59
Black Annie 172
Blue Man 137
Boger 184
Bridge
   400th Avenue 120
   Airtight 142
   Axeman's 82
   Blood's Point 12
   Crybaby 107
   Lakey's Creek 165
   Love Ford 146
   Old Train 106
   Seven Gates 153
   Witch's 112
Brother Otto 45
Burial Mound
   Albany Mounds 21
   Cahokia Mounds 157
   Dickson Mounds 92

Kincaid Mounds 176
Buried Treasure .. 90, 117, 125, 128,
   143, 166, 175, 180
Burrows Cave 182
Burton Cave 89

C

Carbondale Post Office (Former) 168
Cave-In-Rock State Park 166
Cemetery
   "Ragdoll" 142
   Algonquin 47
   Anderson 112
   Archer 70
   Aux Sable 30
   Bachelor's Grove 72
   Bethel 142
   Blood's Point 12
   Bohemian 63
   Calvary 68
   Cemetery X 112
   Centralia 174
   Chesterville 144
   Clements 137
   Cumberland 124
   Elkhart 119
   Elmwood 174
   Graceland 66
   Greenwood 122
   Harrison 163
   Higgins (Coburn) 146
   Lithuanian Liberty 14
   Moon Point 118
   Mound City National 179
   Mount Thabor 47
   Mt. Pleasant 181
   Old Macomb 101
   Old Union 113

Peck 123
Ramsey 114
Resurrection 70
Ridge 131
St. James-Sag 71
St. Omer 140
St. Patrick's 43
White 42
Wigwam Hollow 101
Chanute Air Force Base 136
Chee-Chee-Pin-Quay 73
Chicago Water Tower (old) 61
Church
  Holy Family 59
  Mt. Pleasant 181
  Saint Benedict 62
  St. James-Sag 71
Clark, George Rogers 180
Cohomo 132
College / University
  Barat College (Former) 41
  Benedictine University 77
  Eastern Illinois University 140
  Illinois College 127
  Illinois State University 126
  Knox College 96
  Lewis & Clark College 154
  Lincoln College 120
  McKendree University 158
  Millikin University 122
  North Central College 79
  Rockford College 24
  Southern Illinois University .. 169
  University of Illinois 135
  Western Illinois University .. 100
Cursed Stone, (The) 76
Cyclone Annie 172

D

Death Curve 16
Devil's Bake-Oven 171
Devil's Cave 33
Devil's Gate 42
Diamond Island Phantom 91

Dillinger, John 58
Disaster
  1887 Chatsworth Train Wreck . 117
  1909 Cherry Mine Disaster 13
  1946 Naperville Train Disaster . 78
  1947 Centralia Mine Disaster . 176
  Iroquois Theater Fire 61
  Our Lady of Angels School Fire . 57
  Saint Anthony's Hospital Fire .. 115
Doddridge Farm 43

E

Enfield Horror 186
Excalibur Club 65

F

Farrington Brothers 92
Fox Riverfront 38
Fox Run Subdivision 32

G

Gacy, John Wayne 64
Galena History Museum 17
Giant Skeleton 143
Giant Snake 136
Gooseneck Ghost 98
Gregory, James 175

H

Hartford Castle 155
Haunted Cabin 90, 178
Headless Horseman 165
Herrin Massacre 187
Hickory Hill Plantation 164
High School: *See School*
Home
  Charles Kinney 129
  Crenshaw 164
  Dana-Thomas 129
  Dunham-Hunt 35
  Emma Jones 23
  Frank Shaver Allen 83
  Guiteau 20

Haunting the Illinois | 199

Hundley 169
J. Eldred 116
Jakob Meyer 156
James Nolan 111
John Wayne Gacy (Former) 64
Nellie Dunton 11
Sweetin, The 116
Tycer 141
Vere Cory 32
Horseshoe Mound 17
Hospital
   Ashmore Estates 139
   Choate Mental Health Center . 183
   Manteno State Hospital 80
   Peoria State Hospital 102
   Saint Anthony's Hospital 115
   Sunnybrook 40
Hotel
   Capital Hotel 98
   Congress Plaza Hotel 60
   Drake Hotel 65
   Hotel Baker 36
   Kaskaskia Hotel 44
   Original Springs Hotel 185
   Rose Hotel 167
   Ruebel Hotel 151

I

Independence Grove 42

K

Knox County Jail (Former) 96

L

Lady in Black 97, 172
Lakey's Creek 165
Library
   Elmhurst (Former) 76
   Milner Library 126
   Peoria 105

M

Mansion
   Biszant 155
   Crenshaw 164
   McPike 152
   Wilder 76
   Yates 130
Massock Mausoleum 14
Monk's Mound 157
Monks (phantom) 72
Murphysboro Mud Monster 171

O

Old Slave House 164

P

Pemberton Hall 140
Phantom Steamboat 93
Piasa Lodge 152
Pierson Station 128
Pointing Ghost 19
Pulaski County Courthouse 180
Pyramid State Park 177

R

Read-Dunning Memorial Park 56
Restaurant
   Al Capone's Hideaway and Steak
      House 34
   Country House Restaurant 75
   Friendly Café, The 95
   Maple Tree Inn 54
   Tapestry Room 159
Resurrection Mary 70
Road
   23rd Avenue 19
   Blood's Point Road 12
   Cherry Road 37
   Cole Hollow Road 132
   Cuba Road 42

Dug Hill Road 184
Help Me Road 13
Kennedy Hill Road 18
Lebanon Road 153
Monee Road 82
Munger Road 79
Sangamon Street............... 82
Seventh Avenue Dead End...... 21
Shoe Factory Road 69
Robber's Court 112
Rock Creek Ghost............... 167
Roff, Mary 145

S

Saint Bede Academy 45
School
    Abingdon Middle School (Former).
   94
    Antioch Community High School 39
    Channing Elementary School ... 31
    Charles A. Lindbergh School.... 69
    Fremd High School............. 74
    Illinois State Training School for
        Girls 33
    Joliet Catholic High School
        (Former).................. 83
    Lawrenceville High School ... 173
    Lourdes High School (Former) . 67
    Milton School (Former) 154
    Our Lady of Angels School...... 57
    Quincy Junior High............. 90
    Saint Bede Academy 45
    St. Charles East High School.... 36
    Urbana High School 138
    Yorkville Middle School (Former)..
   38
Seaweed Charlie................. 68
Spoon River 92
Starved Rock State Park.......... 45
Stump Pond Serpent............. 177
Sunnybrook Asylum 40
Sunset Haven................... 170

T

Theater
    Avon Theater................... 121
    Biograph Theater 58
    Chandler Theatre (Former)..... 99
    Coronado Theater.............. 22
    Egyptian Theater............... 29
    Fischer Theatre 147
    Ford Theater................... 61
    Illinois Theatre (Former)....... 99
    Iroquois Theater 61
    Meyer-Jacobs Theatre......... 103
    Oriental Theater 61
    Peoria Players Theatre 104
    Pfeiffer Theater 79
    Rialto Theatre.................. 84
    Ritz Theater 157
Tinker Swiss Cottage............. 24

V

Vampire 14
Violin Annie 174
Vishnu Springs 98

W

Watseka Wonder, The........... 145
Williamsburg Hill............... 131
Willow Creek Farm 15
Witch 43, 85, 112, 118, 140, 144, 172
Woman in White........ 33, 70, 168
Woodhenge.................... 158
Woods
    Effland Woods 94
    LaBaugh Woods................ 63
    Robinson Woods............... 73
    Runyon County Forest Preserve 85
    Twin Sister's Woods............ 25
Woodstock Opera House......... 49
Worth, Mary.................... 43

INDEX BY TOWN AND CITY

Abingdon	94
Albany	21
Algonquin	47
Alton	152
Anna	183
Antioch	39
Ashmore	139
Bartonville	102
Belleville	156
Belvidere	11
Berwyn	53
Blue Island	54
Brookport	176
Browning Township	106
Buckner	163
Burgess Township	111
Burton Township	89
Byron	18
Cambridge	16
Carbondale	168
Cave-In-Rock	166
Centralia	174
Champaign	135
Charleston	140
Chatsworth	117
Cherry	13
Chester	180
Chesterville	144
Chicago	
Bucktown	54
China Town	55
Dunning	56
Edgewater	56
Humboldt Park	57
Lincoln Park	58
Little Italy	59
Loop	60
Near North Side	61
North Center	62
North Park	63
Norwood Park	64
River North	65
Streeterville	65
Uptown	66
West Elsdon	67
Claremont	181
Clarendon Hills	75
Clarksdale	112
Colchester	97
Cold Spring Township	131
Collinsville	153, 157
Crete	82
Creve Coeur	132
Crittenden Township	136
Crystal Lake	47
Danville	147
Decatur	121
Decker Township	182
Dekalb	29
East Alton	154
Effingham	114
Eldred	116
Elgin	31
Elizabethtown	167
Elkhart	119
Elmhurst	76
Enfield	186
Equality	164
Evanston	68
Evans Township	124
Falmouth	146
Farmington	92
Flora Township	12
Freeburg Township	159
Freeport	20
Galena	17

202 | *Michael Kleen*

Galesburg	96
Geneva	32
Glen Ellyn	76
Godfrey	154
Grafton	151
Grand Tower	171
Hardin	91
Hartford	155
Herrin	187
Hoffman Estates	69
Ingleside	40
Jacksonville	127
Joliet	83
Jonesboro	184
Justice	70
Kingston	90
Lake Forest	41
Lake Zurich	42
Lasalle	44
Lawn Ridge	125
Lawrenceville	173
Lebanon	158
Lemont	71
Lewistown	92
Libertyville	42
Lincoln	120
Lisle	77
Lockport	85
Macomb	98
Manteno	80
Mattoon	142
McLeansboro	165
Midlothian	72
Minooka	30
Moline	19
Monmouth	107
Morgan Township	142
Mound City	179
Mount Vernon	172
Murphysboro	171
Naperville	78
New Berlin	129
New Holland	120
Normal	126
Norridge	73
North Aurora	33
Oakley Township	123
Okawville	185
Oswego	37
Palatine	74
Peoria	103
Peru	45
Pyramid State Park	177
Quincy	90
Rantoul	136
Richland County	181
Richmond	48
Rock Creek	167
Rockford	22
Romine Township	175
Shannon	15
Springfield	129
Spring Valley	13
St. Charles	34
Sterling	21
Streator	118
The Gooseneck	178
Tunbridge Township	113
Union Township	143
Unity Township	128
Urbana	137
Utica	45
Vermont	94
Wadsworth	43
Walkerville Township	116
Wamac	176
Watseka	145
Wayne	79
Woodstock	49
Yorkville	38

ABOUT THE AUTHOR

Michael Kleen holds a M.A. in History from Eastern Illinois University and a M.S. in Education from Western Illinois University. He is a freelance columnist, as well as the author of *Haunting Illinois, Paranormal Illinois, Tales of Coles County, Illinois,* and *One Voice,* among other works.

Kleen is also author and publisher of the *Legends and Lore of Illinois,* a monthly newsletter highlighting infamous places in Illinois through a unique blend of research and storytelling. In addition, he regularly writes articles for *KILTER,* the journal of Gothic Art Chicago.

Michael has spoken about local history and folklore at conventions, libraries, cafes, schools, and colleges; and he has presented research papers at the 2007 and 2010 Conference on Illinois History in Springfield. He has also been a guest on several Internet radio shows, "The Mothership Connection" on AM-1050 WLIP, and is a regular guest on the Chicago-based radio program "Thresholds into Other Realms."

Michael is Editor-in-Chief of Untimely Meditations: a Journal of Free Thought and Social Critique, former publisher of *Black Oak Presents,* a quarterly journal of Middle American art and culture, and the proprietor of Black Oak Press, Illinois and Black Oak Media.

www.michaelkleen.com
www.blackoakmedia.org